THE EXISTENTIAL FICTION OF AYI KWEI ARMAH, ALBERT CAMUS, AND JEAN-PAUL SARTRE

Tommie L. Jackson

University Press of America, Inc.
Lanham • New York • London

Library of Congress Cataloging-in-Publication Data

Jackson, Tommie Lee.
The existential fiction of Ayi Kwei Armah, Albert Camus, and Jean-
Paul Sartre / Tommie L. Jackson.
p.   cm.
Includes bibliographical references and index.
1. French fiction--20th century--History and criticism. 2. Ghanaian
fiction (Englilsh)--History and criticism. 3. Existentialism in
literature. 4. Armah, Ayi Kwei, 1939--Criticism and interpretation.
5. Camus, Albert, 1913-1960--Criticism and interpretation. 6.
Sartre, Jean Paul, 1905--Criticism and interpretation. I. Title.
PQ673.J33   1996   823--dc20   96-16218   CIP

ISBN 0-7618-0376-9 (cloth: alk. ppr.)

In memory of my parents, Rev. Thomas Jackson, Jr. and Bertha Clarke Jackson, who instilled in me faith, and to my beloved son, Kofi Ulysses Bofah, who gamely endured my weekend excursions to the library, where I wrestled with the early version of the manuscript. He needs no monument to know how much he is loved.

Copyright   Acknowledgements

A condensed version of chapter two appeared originally as "The Theme of the Absurd in Works by Albert Camus and Ayi Kwei Armah" in *The Griot* 9 (fall, 1990), 13-25. I am grateful to the editor of *The Griot*, Andrew Baskin, for permission to reproduce portions of the article.

Acknowledgements are also due to the following parties for permission to quote from sources:

Robert Fraser. *The Novels of Ayi Kwei Armah.* Copyright (c) 1980 by Robert Fraser. Reprinted by permission of William Heinemann Educational Books, LTD.

Simone Schwarz-Bart. *Between Two Worlds.* Translated by Barbara Bray. Copyright (c) 1981 by Heinemann. Reprinted by permission of the publisher.

Buchi Emecheta. *Destination Biafra.* Copyright (c) 1982 by Buchi Emecheta. Reprinted by permission of Heinemann.

Chinua Achebe. *Things Fall Apart.* Copyright (c) 1959 by Chinua Achebe. Reprinted by permission of Heinemann.

Chinua Achebe. *No Longer at Ease.* Copyright (c) 1960 by Chinua Achebe. Reprinted by permission of Heinemann.

Ayi Kwei Armah. Excerpts from *The Beautyful Ones Are Not Yet Born.* Copyright (c) 1968 by Ayi Kwei Armah. Reprinted by permission of Houghton Mifflin and Company. All rights reserved.

Simone de Beauvoir. *The Mandarins.* Translated by Leonard M. Friedman. Copyright (c) 1981 by W.W. Norton and Company. Reprinted by permission of the publisher.

Simone de Beauvoir. *She Came to Stay.* Copyright (c) 1954 by W.W. Norton and Company. Reprinted by permission of the publisher.

Jean-Paul Sartre. *Nausea.* Translated by Lloyd Alexander. Copyright (c) 1964 by New Directions Publications, Corp. Reprinted by permission of the publisher.

Jean-Paul Sartre. *Intimacy and Other Stories.* Translated by Lloyd Alexander. Copyright (c) 1948 by New Directions Publications, Corp. Reprinted by permission of the publisher.

Albert Camus. *The Rebel: An Essay on Man in Revolt.* Translated by Anthony Bower. Copyright (c) 1956 by Alfred A. Knopf, Inc. Reprinted by permission of the publisher.

Albert Camus. *The Myth of Sisyphus and Other Essays.* Translated by Justin O'Brien. Copyright (c) 1955 by Alfred A. Knopf, Inc. Reprinted by permission of the publisher.

Albert Camus. *The Stranger.* Translated by Stuart Gilbert. Copyright (c) 1946 by Alfred A. Knopf, Inc. Reprinted by permission of the publisher.

Albert Camus. *Resistance, Rebellion and Death.* Translated by Justin O'Brien. Copyright (c) 1960 by Alfred A. Knopf, Inc. Reprinted by permission of the publisher.

Jean-Paul Sartre. *The Age of Reason.* Translated by Eric Sutton. Copyright (c) 1947 by Eric Sutton. Reprinted by permission of Alfred A. Knopf, Inc.

Jean-Paul Sartre. *No Exit.* Translated by Stuart Gilbert. Copyright (c) 1948 by Alfred A. Knopf, Inc. Reprinted by permission of the publisher.

Jean-Paul Sartre. *Existentialism and Humanism.* Translated by Philip Mairet. Copyright (c) 1948 by Methuen and Company. Reprinted by permission of the publisher.

Jean-Paul Sartre. *Being and Nothingness: An Essay on Phenomenological Ontology.* Translated by Hazel E. Barnes. Copyright (c) 1956 by Philosophical Library. Reprinted by permission of the publisher.

Jean-Paul Sartre. *Existential Psychoanalysis.* Translated by Hazel E. Barnes. Copyright (c) 1953 by Philosophical Library. Reprinted by permission of the publisher.

Frantz Fanon. *Black Skin, White Masks.* Translated by Charles Lam Markmann. Copyright (c) 1967 by Grove/Atlantic, Inc. Reprinted by permission of the publisher.

Frantz Fanon. *The Wretched of the Earth.* Translated by Constance Farrington. Copyright (c) 1963 by Grove/Atlantic, Inc. Reprinted by permission of the publisher.

Chinua Achebe. *Morning Yet on Creation Day.* Copyright (c) 1975 by Chinua Achebe. Reprinted by permission of Doubleday.

Contents

Preface

With the advent of the African novel, formally recognized with the publication of Amos Tutuola's *The Palm-Wine Drinkard* in 1951, there have been fervent debates on the especial nature of this literature and the need to establish for it a critical tradition distinct from the Western tradition. The debate has given rise to two fundamental attitudes of criticism. One calls for an orientation which is largely sociological in implication, a cultural view which stresses the need for the critic to be "more of a literary citizen than a literary scholar."[1] One of the chief proponents of this view is Abiola Irele. In the article "The Criticism of Modern African Literature," Irele discusses three aspects of the critical function, based upon Irving Howe's definition of criticism. Irele states that criticism has first the elementary character of being discriminate, "of making reasoned judgements upon literary works based upon fairly clear and definite criteria." He suggests further that criticism is ultimately of a subjective nature since it depends, to a large extent, upon the intuitive responses of the critic as reader. Finally, he asserts that literature takes place within a cultural setting and that there can be no meaningful criticism without the existence of a community of values shared by the writer and the critic, which the latter can in turn make meaningful to the writer's larger audience. On the latter point, Irele argues:

> The quest for coherence in the literary work on purely technical grounds seems to me . . . a dangerous procedure with regard to modern African literature, at least for the moment. What we must look for, I think is the fine balance between art and life, their conjunction in the imaginative creation. I do not hesitate to say, therefore, that as far as the critic of African literature is concerned, he must take the view that literature has no autonomy outside of reality. *The critic of African literature thus has a double responsibility: to show the literary work as a significant statement with a direct relevance to the African experience; and related to this is what I want to call the educative role of criticism in the present context of the literary situation in Africa.* We have a duty not only to make our modern African literature accessible to our people in terms which they can understand, but also in the process, to

promote an understanding of literature, to widen the creative (as well as responsive) capabilities of our people—the two essential elements in a fruitful literary life. (Italics mine.)[2]

The upshot of Irele's reasoning is that the critic of African literature has the vital functions of educating his African reading public in order to foster a healthy literary community and of correlating the literature to its cultural milieu in order to reveal the historical consciousness of the people.

The implications of this third point, which defines the role of the critic as a kind of middleman between the writer and his reading public, have raised questions concerning the nature and function of African criticism. Some interpret this response to literature as an ingenuous acceptance of mediocre works, an acknowledgement of the imperative that "if a work is of sufficient sociological or historical interest, then we can dispense with literary criteria for evaluation."[3] Others perceive the ethnological concerns, combined with a vehement display of hostility against the Western-styled critic, as a chauvinistic concept which has its footing in "Africanism" and challenge, on these grounds, the integrity of the approach.[4] The conjectural nature of Irele's article makes difficult any attempt to approve generously these arguments. It does appear, however, that what has emerged under the name of sociological criticism has given sufficient support to these claims and has increased doubt among skeptics as to the viability of the approach. The subsequent reviews of Ernest Emenyonu and Harold Collins should serve to illustrate this point.

In the article "Who Does Flora Nwapa Write For?" Emenyonu challenges the remark made by Adeola James that "considering her [Nwapa's] performance in both *Efuru* and *Idu* one cannot help wondering what motivates Miss Nwapa beyond the elementary wish of everyone to be a writer."[5] Emenyonu argues his defense by offering critical perspectives which recall those of Irele. He observes that the critic has "an obligation to society. . . . He should identify the content, the traditional content in each case. He should show what the author has done with the traditional material, and how he has changed traditional forms to fit modern conditions."[6] Having stated this proposition, Emenyonu goes on to champion the "peculiar realism" in *Idu*, the phenomenon which he describes as *Ume:*

Tragedy in the Igbo situation is not in the feeling that nothing goes right for the individual, but the fact that any success he attains is followed sooner or later by a bigger and more terrible misfortune. This is a constant reality in Igbo life, which among some Igbo groups is described as the phenomenon of *Ume.*[7]

Emenyonu places unqualified emphasis on peripheral matters but does not come to terms with the crux of the problem. The criticism James had made in her review was that the novel *Idu* had "failed to grip." This she attributed to two serious faults in the novel: the novel's thematic uncertainty and the author's inability to dramatize a potentially serious theme--the importance of children in an African marriage. Emenyonu gives only cursory attention to these remarks by James. Instead, Emenyonu credits Nwapa for "the realism of her themes and her ever increasing sensitive use of language."[8]

Whether or not this defense can be made is irrelevant to the debate. What is relevant is how effectively Nwapa has rendered her particular vision to reflect an African system of values. Because Emenyonu does not show how these traditional elements forward the meaning of the novel, how they intensify its value, he comes dangerously close to writing a social and historical commentary and to fashioning a *reductio ad absurdum* of Irele's critical postulate.

Another critic, Harold Collins, posing as one of the few defenders of Amos Tutuola, adopts a stance similar to Emenyonu's in the article "Founding a New National Literature." The critic, responding to the critical indictments summarized by John V. Murra,[9] tries to establish the merit of *The Palm-Wine Drinkard* based on genetic criteria. For example, he considers the characters in the novel both "credible" and "substantial" and argues their genesis in Yoruba folklore:

> Drinkard is clearly established as a shrewd, witty, easy-going Yoruba. The wanderer in the bush of ghosts, very like Drinkard though explicitly distinguished from him, is even slightly more credible in that he usually exercises his wit and pluck without the almost inexhaustible store of ju-ju that Drinkard has at his command.[10]

Collins also describes Tutuola's language as "a perpetual delight" and remarks that "for all the crudity of language, we are as much struck by the clarity, directness, vigor, and felicity of this Anglo-Nigerian language of Tutuola's as we are by its unconventionality."[11]

Similar to Emenyonu's, the plaudit Tutuola receives from Collins stems from a non-standard dialect and an analogous portrayal of traditional characters. A cultural explanation, by the critic, to reveal the social patterns of the literature is acceptable; but to judge the literature, as Collins does here, primarily on the merit of its "realness," or the verisimilitude of language, is to foster, perhaps unwittingly, the conceits criticized by opponents. This corrupt form of criticism is apparently what Nigerian author Wole Soyinka was addressing when he stated in an interview:

The greatest lack I think quite frankly is criticism. We have not at the moment got
good critics in Nigeria, and European foreign critics are not helping by being
Eurocentrically condescending, applying a different standard for writing.[12]

The exaggerated form which sociological criticism has taken, has, in
fact, belied its purpose. The view articulated by Irele is that literature
is a vehicle of culture. The critical standards which define it must by
nature be suited to its object. African literature is currently being
judged by a foreign audience which subscribes almost wholly to the
values adopted from the Western tradition. The result is an esthetic
which accepts, in theory, the literature as a tributary of European
literature and which interprets the literature in light of its own realities.
Such a narrow view is, according to some, destined to prove itself
inadequate. Chinua Achebe purports that "a national literature is one
that takes the whole nation for its province and has a realized or
potential audience throughout its territory. Any attempt to define
African literature in terms which overlook the complexities of the
African scene is doomed to failure."[13] Similarly, Solomon Iyasere
concedes that the Eurocentric canon has "'liberated' African literature
from the strong grips of cultural anthropologists," but notes that "it has
failed to respond adequately to the nuances of African fiction."[14]
On the other hand, the disagreement from opponents has not sprung
from the advocacy of more relative critical standards. Eustace Palmer,
for instance, agrees that the linguistic burden of the writer and the
essential newness of the literature make necessary some critical
allowances.[15] The disagreement has come rather with the wholesale
acceptance of the second critical function as postulated by Irele--that of
bringing the literature home to its reading public and of demonstrating
the relevance of the literature to African culture and society. As a result
of this proposed critical perspective by Irele, sociological critics have
rushed to the defense of writers who imbue their works with cultural
information and, at the expense of literary excellence, have provided
acceptance for such writers. This practice in criticism connotes
partisanship and confirms the suspicion amongst skeptics that the merit
of a work hinges upon the number of social references the critic can
abstract from the literature.
It is no accident, for example, that the reviews of Adeola James and
Eldred Jones on Flora Nwapa are concurrent. In the article "Locale and
Universe--Three Nigerian Novels," Jones makes the assessment that
there is no lack of cultural information in the novel *Efuru*, but contends
that what is absent in the novel is a definitive purpose and a solid
advancement of any major theme. He writes:

What Flora Nwapa's novel lacks is a strong overall conception apart from the obvious urge to show how Ibos live. Incidents seem to be devised with this in mind rather than to advance any major theme. One is at a loss to understand, for example, what the purpose of the author is in introducing into a market a lady in European dress, except perhaps to show that Ibo women who have never been to school do not understand English. This woman disappears as mysteriously as she had first appeared. This gratuitous episode, like a number of others, contributes little to the novel as a whole.[16]

The criticism made here reveals a precarious handling of subject material by the author which later manifests itself in the disjointedness of the novel. This insight, because it coincides with James' earlier view of "trivia" and "thematic uncertainty" by the author, has to be taken seriously. Emenyonu, by attempting on grounds of realism to eradicate these charges, betrays his own partisanship and demonstrates the extent to which critics can be driven if influenced by nationalistic ideology.

In similar fashion, Chinweizu, Onwuchekwa Jemie, and Ihechukwu Madubuike identify the extent to which authors borrow from African orature as one standard of measure for African prose and poetry. Subsequently, Tutuola's work receives praise for its linguistic experimentation:

Here we should mention the successes of Tutuola and the Onitsha market writers in producing their works in the variants of English used in their respective milieux. Instead of applauding them and administering sympathetic criticism that is compatible with these writers' aims, some African critics have expressed embarrassment and hostility at Tutuola's "bad English" (or "young English," as Dylan Thomas called it), and would on that account prefer to see such works excluded from the body of "serious" African literature.[17]

It appears, however, that this direction in criticism is the result of the "roots" philosophy as articulated by Irele. That is to say, the emphasis on national consciousness and the view of African literature as a literature apart from world culture and its imposed critical standards has quickly developed into a school of thought which approaches literature almost entirely on ethnic grounds. This tendency, because it misrepresents literature and reduces it to social documents, has to be eschewed. This is not, however, to discount the value of sociological interpretations. Such an approach provides channels for exploring the literature by first of all giving it context. But sociological criticism should supplement, not substitute itself, for more formal analysis. As Solomon Iyasere has maintained:

The information about cultural background is simply information, descriptive and not evaluative. Of itself, it does not elucidate the work. As information, it can be ascertained by any careful study. But when we apply this as an aid in explicating a text, we move from the descriptive to the analytical and evaluative, and it is here that the literary critic's task begins.[18]

1. D. Ibe Nwoga, "The Limitations of Universal Critical Criteria," *Dalhousie Review* 53 (1973-74): 629.

2. Abiola Irele, "The Criticism of Modern African Literature," in *Perspectives on African Literature*, ed. Christopher Heywood (New York: Africana Publishing Corporation, 1971), 23.

3. Eustace Palmer, "The Criticism of African Fiction: Its Nature and Function," *The International Fiction Review* 1 (July 1974): 113.

4. Solomon Iyasere, "African Critics on African Literature—A Study in Misplaced Hostility," *The Journal of Modern African Studies* 12 (Sept. 1974): 515.

5. Adeola James, review of *Idu*, by Flora Nwapa, *African Literature Today* 5 (1971): 152.

6. Ernest Emenyonu, "Who Does Flora Nwapa Write For?," *African Literature Today* 7 (1975): 33.

7. Ibid., 31.

8. Ibid., 32.

9. John Murra, "The Unconscious of a Race," review of *The Palm-Wine Drinkard* and *My Life in the Bush* by Amos Tutuola, *Nation* 179 (Sept. 1954): 261-62.

10. Harold Collins, "Founding a New National Literature," *Critique: Studies in Modern Fiction* 4 (1960-61): 19.

11. Ibid., 18-19.

12. Cosmo Pieterse and Dennis Duerden, *African Writers Talking: A Collection of Radio Interviews* (New York: Africana Publishing Corporation, 1972), 176.

13. Chinua Achebe, "The African Writer and the English Language," in *Morning Yet on Creation Day: Essays* (New York: Anchor Press, 1976), 92-93.

14. Solomon Iyasere, "The Place of Oral Tradition in the Criticism of African Literature," *Books Abroad* 49 (winter 1975): 51.

15. Palmer, "The Criticism of African Fiction," 112.

16. Eldred Jones, "Locale and Universe—Three Nigerian Novels," *The Journal of Commonwealth Literature* 3 (1967): 129.

17. Chinweizu, Onwuchekwa Jemie, and Ihechukwu Madubuike, *Toward the Decolonization of African Literature, vol 1, African Fiction and Poetry and Their Critics* (Washington, D.C.: Howard UP, 1983), 263-64.

18. Solomon Iyasere, "African Critics on African Literature—A Study in Misplaced Hostility," *The Journal of Modern African Studies* 12 (Sept. 1974): 517.

Acknowledgements

I wish to express my deep sense of gratitude to Professor Oyekan Owomoyela, University of Nebraska-Lincoln, who supervised my graduate work on African literature and ignited my interest in African literature; the reference librarians at St. Cloud State University, St. Cloud, Minnesota, who worked assiduously to acquire some of the needed resources for this study; the administration at St. Cloud State University who, by granting me a year-long sabbatical during the academic year 1995-96, afforded me the time needed in order to prepare this study for publication; and, finally, Michelle Harris, Acquisitions Editor, and Helen Hudson, Production Editor, University Press of America, for guiding this work through production.

Introduction

Emile Snyder, in an article published in 1972, distinguished between two groups of African writers. On the one hand, there was the first generation of writers epitomized by Chinua Achebe and Cyprian Ekwensi and, on the other, the second generation epitomized by Ayi Kwei Armah and Wole Soyinka. According to Snyder, the first generation of writers "conceived of a reality in the same manner in which the traditional English novelists conceived of it. That is, reality is one, cohesive: it can be described."[1] With regard to the novel *Things Fall Apart* by Chinua Achebe, Synder noted:

> The action unfolds in a linear manner, in a chronological fashion: it conforms to the biography of the characters in the novels. The tempo of Okonkwo's life, in *Things Fall Apart*–from youth to maturity and death--coincides with the narrative movement, from the rise of the hero to his disgrace and reconquered dignity in death. Indeed one might argue that *Things Fall Apart* reflects some of the Aristotlean tenets of tragedy. The tragedy of the Ibo people, the falling apart of the clan, unfold in the chronological succession of years. Time and space, that is history and geography, are indivisible from the particular fate of the characters.[2]

Contrastingly, the novels by the writers of the second generation, particularly those by Wole Soyinka, are seen by Snyder as "breaking with the purely historical and societal concerns of past Nigerian novels, breaking with the conception of plots and characters in a novel." Snyder notes that "with *The Interpreters* the African novel transcends history and enters into the realm of metaphysics."[3]

The point, as being made by Snyder, is that the works by the first generation of writers are steeped in historical reality and are by nature more concerned with historical truth and verisimilitude. By contrast, the works by the second generation of writers are ahistorical, their movement more towards what Snyder refers to as "the collective consciousness of history into the consciousness of a single human being."[4] To illustrate, Snyder notes the impersonalization of some of the authors' fictional heroes. For example, the man in *The Beautyful Ones Are Not Yet Born* is simply designated as "the man," indicating that he is to serve a symbolic function in the novel. He not only embraces the particular moral dilemma which many Ghanaians experienced following their country's independence but, more collectively, his isolation reflects that of many whose morality puts them sorely out of step with those whose values are indecent and corrupt. It is because of this mythic comparison, or of "man's *déracinement* in a world which moves too fast, too mechanically, to fix the human personality and its history" that Snyder notes "the novels of the second generation of African writers remind us more of the works of Kafka, Malraux, Camus, and Beckett than of the traditional English novelists."[5]

The parallel of these second generation writers, particularly Ayi Kwei Armah, to French existentialism and to the modern experimental novel has also been made by Richard Priebe. Classifying African writers on the basis of their "common sensibility," Priebe sees the literature of Chinua Achebe as representative of an "ethical consciousness" whose development favors realism, specificity in time and place, and chronology. On the other hand, Priebe considers the literature of Ayi Kwei Armah as representative of a "mythic consciousness" where the development is largely symbolic and ahistorical. Because the literature of Ayi Kwei Armah often transcends a particular time and place, unlike the literature of Chinua Achebe which is often strongly ensconced in the traditional, Priebe finds the work of Ayi Kwei Armah more easily "seen in terms of European existentialism and Frantz Fanon's philosophy regarding the colonized individual" than "with traditional African myths and rituals."[6]

Despite the frequency of the association of the Ghanaian author with French existentialism, however, it was not until Shelby Steele's article "Existentialism in the Novels of Ayi Kwei Armah"[7] that the correlation was developed in any sustained form. Noting specifically the themes of alienation, malaise, and emotional apathy, Steele had argued the correlation of Ayi Kwei Armah to the French existentialists, Camus and Sartre; however, once again, perhaps due to the constraints of the article publication, the impression was that the critic was "breaking ground," since Steele's treatment of the themes was more expository than analytical, thus suggesting an incidental rather than a philosophical parallel.

The purpose of this study, therefore, will be to amplify and to extend the parallels as they have been noted by the various critics. Toward that end, the writer, after a review of Armahian criticism to date, will explore in five successive chapters the existential themes as they predominantly emerge from the novels of Ayi Kwei Armah. Those themes are the Absurd in *The Beautyful Ones Are Not Yet Born;* the Other in *The Beautyful Ones Are Not Yet Born* and *Fragments;* the Self-Flagellation and Narcissism of the Intellectual Hero in *Fragments* and *Why Are We So Blest?;* Revolution versus Revolt in *Why Are We So Blest?* and *Two Thousand Seasons;* and the author's Emergent Pacifism in *The Healers.* The final chapter will examine Armah's oeuvre in the context of other African authors and will seek to draw some conclusions on the future direction of the author and his literature.

1. Emile Snyder, "New Directions in African Writings," *Pan-African Journal* 5 (1972): 255.

2. Ibid., 254-55.

3. Ibid., 256.

4. Ibid., 256.

5. Ibid., 256-57.

6. Richard Priebe, "The Development of a Mythic Consciousness in West African Literature" (Ph.D. dissertation, University of Texas at Austin, 1973), vi.

7. Shelby Steele, "Existentialism in the Novels of Ayi Kwei Armah," *Obsidian: Black Literature in Review* 3 (spring 1977): 5-13.

Chapter 1

A Survey of Critical Opinion
on Armah's Fiction

Despite the publication to date of five novels--*The Beautyful Ones Are Not Yet Born* (1968), *Fragments* (1970), *Why Are We So Blest?* (1972), *Two Thousand Seasons* (1973), and *The Healers* (1978)--Ayi Kwei Armah remains one of the most enigmatic and controversial of the Anglophone African authors. The elusiveness is attributable in part to an expressed reluctance to engage in dialogue with his reading public. Mistaken assumptions are the end result which, occasionally, compel the writer to break his silence in order to reply, as in the article "One Writer's Education."

Ayi Kwei Armah calls to task Ojong Oyuk and, implicitly, Robert Fraser for the biographical information contained in the latter's *The Novels of Ayi Kwei Armah*. The writer takes umbrage to Ayuk's classification of him as a protégé of Frantz Fanon, responding that "This is flattering but untrue. That Fanon's work influenced my thinking is a matter of course. But intense as the contact was, it was purely intellectual, not personal."[1]

The author likewise chafes at the statements made by Ayuk, influenced by Fraser's work, that he spent "several years" as a high school student in America rather than one at Groton, the Massachusetts prep school, and that he graduated from Harvard summa cum laude with a B.A. in Sociology. Analogous to Modin Dofu, the character in *Why Are We So Blest?* who is a fictional representation of Armah, Armah had left Harvard in 1963, a year prior to graduation in order to participate in the struggle for African liberation. In his words,

1

I left Harvard before the official end of my undergrad studies because concurrently with my academic work I'd been trying to decide what my lifework was to be. By the beginning of my final year I had decided, if possible, to work with the liberation movements in southern Africa, all involved, from my perspective, in the same fundamental process.[2]

In another article, "The Lazy School of Literary Criticism," published in 1984, Armah had explained that his refusal to grant interviews is due to the exigencies of time and his belief that "textual spadework" is the responsibility of the critic.[3] Needless to say, the author's reluctance to discuss his writing has not only led to occasional false reportage but has fueled speculation that Armah not only is an alienated writer, but is a misanthrope. Ben Obumselu in the article "Marx, Politics and the African Novel" writes that "It is hardly an exaggeration to describe Armah's alienation from his countrymen on his return after many years in America as a misanthropic neurosis" [4] and goes on to argue that it is the author's estrangement, coupled with his uncommon views, which call into question his role as the "socialist defender of the reality of the common people."[5]

The ironic divide between Armah and those he professes to represent is reminiscent of the one noted by Richard Wright in *Black Boy* wherein he alluded to the Communist agitators as operating in a void.[6] To be sure, the penchant for creating intellectual types has led to the branding of Armah as an elitist whose fictional reality does not reflect common experience. As Derek Wright has observed with respect to the fifth and, implicitly, Armah's other novels:

> . . . the individuals whom these illuminati [healers] elect to heal seem always to be drawn from the higher echelons of society. Unwilling that seed should be sown in infertile ground, the aristocratic elite in charge of Armah's healing mission reserves its therapeutic energies for those of royal (Araba) and noble (Asamoa) birth. The healing of division is itself a divisive process.[7]

The "explicit recognition of a special role for the artist/intellectual in Armah's later works" Richard Peck likewise sees as an example of Ayi Kwei Armah's alienation:

> To judge from the content of his novels, Armah remains thoroughly alienated from his society, although he maintains his commitment to the eventual curing of that society. He has found a community (or hopes that he may do so) not in the community of the common people where Ngugi has found his, but in the community of the uncommon—the committed artists and intellectuals of Africa. (40)[8]

Armah's transplantation from Ghana to other parts of the African continent has not lessened the controversy or charges against him of philosophical estrangement from those whose cause he professes to champion. Time spent by the author in Algeria and Tanzania has led to the conclusion by some that the author has exiled himself from his homeland. An inspection of *Fragments, Two Thousand Seasons,* and *The Healers* reveals, however, that the opposite is true; that his African travels are endemic of the attitude that all of Africa is his homeland: "I do not even think I am in a foreign country as long as I am here in Africa."[9]

In addition to the author's alleged ideological estrangement, criticism of the author has been related to his vision of Africa, as it has been articulated in his works. Charles E. Nnolim in his article "Dialectic as Form: Pejorism in the Novels of Armah" classifies Armah as a pessimist identifiable with the Goncourts, Walter Pater, Paul Verlaine, and Joseph Conrad because of his hopelessly gloomy outlook on life: "Armah is a writer whose creative vision reveals a delight with scenes of defeat, frustration, disappointment, loss. He is a writer whose philosophic pessimism is undisguised in each work."[10] Given the preponderance of images of filth, decay, and putrefaction contained in *The Beautyful Ones Are Not Yet Born,* Nnolim concludes that although Armah is a bold writer, he lacks the class of Chinua Achebe who in *A Man of the People* was able to make effectively the same point of a corrupt body politic:

> One must express revulsion at the insensitivity in Armah's language in which there is a lack of discriminating taste and, one must say, a lack of class. Achebe, in *A Man of the People,* accomplished much of what Armah tried to do in *The Beautyful Ones Are Not Yet Born* with respect to the body politic and their respective countries.[11]

Integral to the author's "warped" social vision is the propensity to create characters who are caricatures rather than recognizable human beings. Of the timber merchant who in *The Beautyful Ones* is indistinguishable from his "ravenous teeth," Obumselu argues,

> The mode is caricature, but caricature in which the artist is determined that the exaggerated strokes will not add up to any kind of identity. Armah's description of persons pays attention to the social trappings, cars, gowns, perfumes, trinkets, shirts, and voices sometimes, but never to character or to that obscure intuition of it which we receive, or think we do, from people's faces."[12]

Obumselu's argument of caricature is echoed by Leonard Kibera in the article "Pessimism and the African Novelist: Ayi Kwei Armah's *The Beautyful Ones Are Not Yet Born"* wherein he describes Armah's fictional approach as "caricature, that refuge of the cartoonist who is pressed for time."[13] This brush-stroke characterization, in the view of Kibera, reduces the novel to the level of moral fable.

Thin characterization, in the view of Derek Wright, is matched by an undefined setting in the third novel *Why Are We So Blest?*. Contrasting the novel with Armah's early fiction, Wright finds the design "diagrammatic" and the symbolism "single-minded telegraphese,"[14] both of which are evident in the author's creation of a fictional No Man's Land:

> They [Aimée and Modin] arrive in a nowhere which is everywhere, a white landscape in which everything, like themselves, is the same. The setting is a mere prop for poetic concepts, a backdrop for symbols: the novel has taken flight into the region of pure metaphor.[15]

William Lawson in his work *The Western Scar*, also criticizes the obscurity of place in *Why Are We So Blest?*, which he considers indicative of the thesis-ridden nature of the work. He has written in *The Western Scar:*

> Perhaps Armah would have done well to have avoided the ambiguity and confusion of his fictional African settings. One is not certain if the action occurs in North Africa or West Africa. Some descriptions suggest that Afrasia is the fictional counterpart of Algeria, but the characters are black, sub-Suharan Africans. One cannot be certain whether Aimée and Modin move north or south as they travel into the desert. Clarifying these details, however, is obviously not Armah's concern. He wishes to oppose a stereotypic idea of Africa against stereotypic ideas of the West. So contradictions and uncertainties in his setting do not deter him. Setting only serves to provide places where action and theme can merge.[16]

One of the most damning reviews of Armah's fiction, however, comes from Adewale Maja-Pearce. Pearce takes exception to James Booth who describes *Why Are We So Blest?* in his article *"Why Are We So Blest?* and the Limits of Metaphor" as "the most powerful work of a novelist of genius."[17] According to Pearce, critics such as Booth do African literature a disservice by promoting mediocrity and, implicitly, the racist tenets of the novel that are inscribed on the female character Aimée who is depicted as inhuman: "Those critics and academics who are busy trying to reassure mediocre writers that they are producing masterpieces are the greatest enemies of Africa today."[18]

A more measured tone is adopted by Bernth Lindfors in his article "Armah's Histories." Lindfors, in his discussion of Armah's latter two novels, observes the contrast between *Two Thousand Seasons, The Healers* and the writer's earlier works: "Instead of witnessing the anguish of a doomed, fragmented individual, we are shown the joy of a mini tribe united in the struggle against evil. Instead of existential despair, there is revolutionary hope. Instead of defeat, victory."[19] Lindfors also compares, unfavorably, Armah's *The Healers* with Chinua Achebe's *Things Fall Apart* and *Arrow of God.* Comparable to Achebe's two novels, *The Healers* is fictionalized history. Nonetheless, Achebe's account of Africa's history is, in Lindfors' estimation, more realistic; also, less inflammatory than is Armah's:

> In *Things Fall Apart* and *Arrow of God* Achebe shows us complex human beings entangled in a web of circumstances that ultimately brings disaster to rural Igbo society. The individuals portrayed cannot be divided into two camps--the saints versus the sinners--but rather can be recognized as quite ordinary people motivated by fairly commonplace ambitions and desires. Moreover, the communities in which they live are not perfect or even remotely perfectable; they are rift with conflicts ranging from the petty to the profound, conflicts which are exacerbated when an alien civilization intrudes into their relatively encapsulated world. The ensuing interaction between Europe and Africa is not really a species of all-out war but rather an uneasy, and at times unpeaceful, coexistence of differing world-views in which the inability of one side to comprehend the perspective of the other precipitates tragedy. Achebe perceives that it was a failure of communication, not an absence of humanity, that was responsible for certain of the catastrophes of the colonial period. In documenting the numerous ironies of this confused era with such compassion and lucidity, Achebe proves a more convincing historian than Armah. Achebe deeply understands ethnocentrism, whereas Armah shallowly advocates it.[20]

He also criticizes the facile assumptions on which the optimism of *Two Thousand Seasons* is based--"that entire races of people can be reduced to the level of primal forces, that one can be characterized as inherently predisposed towards good, another addicted to evil"--and accuses Armah of advocating in *Two Thousand Seasons* a philosophy of "paranoia, an anti-racist racism."[21]

Wole Soyinka in *Myth, Literature and the African World* defends *Two Thousand Seasons* from the attack of racism, responding that its criticism of alien contamination is "a preparatory exercise for the liberation of the mind."[22] He does, however, identify as a weakness in the novel the non-specificity of 'the Way': "'The Way' remains a hazy and undefined ideology; it is the action that defines it, and the guiding principles debated by the protagonists."[23] Likewise, Derek Wright has been critical of the non-specificity of 'The Way':

> The presentation of the ideology of the Way is . . . marked by a vagueness of definition and a disregard for concrete particulars and the quick of experience which are quite alien to the oral tradition. The interminable repetition of the Way's sacred trinity of neologisms--"reciprocity", "connectedness" and "creation"--is accompanied by so little explication of what they practically involve as a lived social pattern that they eventually become lifeless verbal tags, self-enclosed abstractions which fail to translate into anything beyond themselves.[24]

Echoing Wright's criticism of *Two Thousand Seasons* is Eustace Palmer who has written in his article "Negritude Rediscovered: A Reading of the Recent Novels of Armah, Ngugi, and Soyinka":

> There is much talk in *Two Thousand Seasons* about the ideals and values of "the way"; a lot of our information about it comes through the mouths of prophetesses and seers, but there is little actual demonstration of "the way" in action, most of the book being taken up, in fact, by the attempts of the virtuous to rediscover "the way" after the disasters of colonialism and postcolonialism. Furthermore, one is not quite certain that Armah has succeeded in his intention of convincing us that the destruction of values associated with "the way" was entirely the responsibility of the white destroyers.[25]

Criticism has also sprung from the Utopian vision of *Two Thousand Seasons.* Chinyere Nwahunanya has written in the article "A Vision of the Ideal: Armah's *Two Thousand Seasons:* "He [Armah] digs into the past, retrieves an almost lost gem, 'the way,' and presents it as the most viable option open to the Africa of the future. It is a call for a return to a lost Eden."[26]

The influence of the African oral tradition on *Two Thousand Seasons* and *The Healers* has been remarked by critics. Edward Sackey in his article "Oral Tradition and the African Novel" has maintained that the narration of *Two Thousand Seasons,* from the perspective of the twenty initiates, is indicative of the novel's theme of communalism. In his words,

> We know that the narrators are the group of twenty freedom fighters or revolutionaries. There has to be a spokesman for the group; he speaks for and on behalf of the group. He exists in the fictional world of the novel. His voice is heard loud and clear. But his identity is hidden. The explanation could be what is important is the communal identity, not the individual identity; the individual identity is therefore subordinated to the communal identity.[27]

The participatory nature of *Two Thousand Seasons,* as evidenced by questions such as "Who is it calling for examples?," the incantatory nature of the prose, its element of tricksterism, as borrowed from the various African trickster tales, and the epic quality of the novel are considered by Sackey as examples of elements of the African oral tradition. On the latter characteristic, Sackey has written:

> *Two Thousand Seasons* is encyclopedic in structure in the sense that it is a storehouse of knowledge about Africa. Indeed, Armah's deep knowledge of African cultural traditions is brought to the fore in the novel. It contains the history, literature, languages, philosophy, geography, biology, government, law, and politics of traditional Africa. The novel is ... multigeneric in a limited sense; thus, it can be said to be an African epic that has its roots in the oral tradition of Africa.[28]

Despite the differences both in tone and in the narrative construct of *Two Thousand Seasons, The Healers* and Armah's first three novels, Armah's oeuvre can be linked thematically. For example, *Why Are We So Blest?* presages *Two Thousand Seasons* in its revolutionary credo to seek the destruction of the destroyers.[29] Indeed, Derek Wright finds the basic paradigms in Armah's fiction, as evidenced in *Two Thousand Seasons*--"exiled visionaries, healing creators, dictators who exist by the apathetic permission of their intellectual superiors, parasitical potentates who desire only to live in old slave-castles and cover their emptiness with materialism"--as tending toward the tautologous.[30]

Even Armah's early short stories anticipate themes in his novels. "Yaw Manu's Charm,"[31] published prior to *The Beautyful Ones Are Not Yet Born*, contains one of Armah's recurrent themes, namely, the destructive impact of neo-colonialism which is illuminated by Yaw Manu, whose religious indoctrination drives him to put complete faith in prayer in order to pass the examination that will eventually earn him admission to Achimota, one of Ghana's famous secondary schools and, incidentally, Ayi Kwei Armah's alma mater. Although Yaw Manu was among the group of boys to pass the examination and gain admission to the secondary school, his devoutness, ironically, may have, according to the narrator, prevented him from passing later the Cambridge School Certificate Examination (92).

Even when Yaw Manu accepts a job at the British Bank of West Africa where the narrator has also secured employment, he is not deterred from his dream of attending Cambridge. In fact, Yaw Manu, in light of his acquisitions, namely, the panaceas of European origin, appears to have embraced everything European in his pursuit of the elusive success (93).

After repeated failures to pass the examination, Yaw Manu's indebtedness, which is caused by expenditures on "charms," lead him to take desperate measures, namely, the attempted robbery of the British Bank of West Africa, his place of employment. He had been duped by a maalam into believing that a charm costing twenty-five pounds would make him invisible to his would-be captors. Through implicit irony, Armah reveals how Yaw Manu's desire to become an *assimilado* had precipitated his own destruction. This theme of self-destructive self-hatred, or masochism, as developed in a later chapter in this work, is extended in his third novel *Why Are We So Blest?*.

The condition of schizophrenia, caused by the split between two cultures, creates the ambivalence in Armah's fiction. Solo's paralysis in *Why Are We So Blest?* is caused in part by his attraction to Western art, or to that which damns him.[32] Many critics have elected to see in the creation of character a representative of the author himself.

Norman Albritton Spencer in his dissertation "Political Consciousness and Commitment in Modern African Literature: A Study of the Novels of Ayi Kwei Armah" draws a parallel between Ayi Kwei Armah and his fictional characters:

> [Armah] was suffering from the same alienation and fragmented sensibility that his characters struggle so desperately to overcome. Like them, he had been subjected to the dehumanizing tendencies of a modern world capitalist system dominated by the West, and as a result he was disconnected from the harmonious, integrated relations that exist in the organic, communalistic society of traditional Africa. For him, the outer world appears alien and threatening. What remains is his own colonized psyche, trapped, turned inward, thwarted in its attempt to discover a viable mode of transcendence.[33]

As revealed in *Why Are We So Blest?* and in "Yaw Manu's Charm," the schizophrenia of the *assimilado* is often the product of a Western education. Concomitant to their divided loyalties is a profound alienation and despair which give to Armah's fiction a distinct existential quality. Needless to say, Armah's concern in his literature with "the human condition" has sparked criticism from some corners; more specifically, from Chinua Achebe, who finds the despair of some recent fiction indicative of "the near-pathological eagerness to contract the sicknesses of Europe in a horribly mistaken belief that our claim to sophistication is improved thereby."[34] Subsequently, he finds the Ghana represented in *The Beautyful Ones* "unrecognizable" because of the author's attempt to transport "foreign metaphor" onto an African canvas.[35] Indeed, the existentialist parallels that Achebe notes in his article "Africa and Her Writers" have been echoed elsewhere. Norman Spencer has asserted that

> A comparison between Armah in *The Beautyful Ones* and a wide range of European authors from Dostoevsky to Sartre can be carried further. The same oppressive social conditions and "degraded values" that transform men and women into isolated and disoriented individuals who lack a sustaining sense of community exists simultaneously in the West and in the Third World. Therefore, when Armah writes a novel in which characters function as disoriented and passive voyeurs and social relations correspond to chaotic market principles of exchange, he is describing a phenomenon that is not limited only to Europe and to North America.[36]

Similarly, Taban lo Liyong has summarized in the article "Ayi Kwei Armah in Two Moods" the themes shared in common with the French existentialists Sartre and Camus:

> The bravado with which Modin left Harvard, just as the quixoticism with which Armah left Harvard, are existential manifestations. The madness that Baako experienced in *Fragments* exemplifies existential aloneness. Also, the heat of the

Algerian sun and desert which brings out the worst characteristics in man, had already been remarked upon by Albert Camus, another existential darling of the American campuses of the sixties. Especially in his plays, Sartre never tired of showing that intense company is hell. Three sisters; a man, his sister and mother, as in *Fragments* of Armah, are proofs of the philosophy. Or the pressure of the family, on behalf of the bigger, wider society, on the family head--'the man' in *The Beautyful Ones.*[37]

These themes of man's estrangement from the universe and man's contention with those who would circumscribe his freedom are, respectively, the subject of chapters two and three of this work.

10   Existential Fiction

1. Ayi Kwei Armah, "One Writer's Education," *West Africa*, 26 August 1985, 1752.

2. Ibid., 1752.

3. Ayi Kwei Armah, "The Lazy School of Literary Criticism," *West Africa*, 25 February 1985, 353.

4. Ben Obumselu, "Marx, Politics and the African Novel," *20th Century Studies, The Third World: Tensions of Independence* 10 (December 1973): 114.

5. Ibid., 116.

6. Richard Wright, *Black Boy (American Hunger): A Record of Childhood and Youth* (New York: Harper Perennial, 1993), 346.

7. Derek Wright, *Ayi Kwei Armah's Africa: The Sources of His Fiction* (London: Hans Zell Publishers, 1989), 264.

8. Richard Peck, "Hermits and Saviors, Osagyefos and Healers: Artists and Intellectuals in the Works of Ngugi and Armah," *Research in African Literatures* 20, no. 1 (1989): 40.

9. Ode S. Ogede, "Angled Shots and Reflections: On the Literary Essays of Ayi Kwei Armah," *World Literature Today* 66 (summer 1992): 442.

10. Charles E. Nnolim, "Dialectic as Form: Pejorism in the Novels of Armah," *African Literature Today: Retrospect and Prospect* 10 (1979): 207.

11. Ibid., 223.

12. Obumselu, 115.

13. Leonard Kibera, "Pessimism and the African Novelist: Ayi Kwei Armah's *The Beautyful Ones Are Not Yet Born,*" *The Journal of Commonwealth Literature* 4 (1979): 67.

14. Derek Wright, 190.

15. Ibid., 192-93.

16. William Lawson, *The Western Scar: The Theme of the Been-to in West African Fiction* (Athens, Ohio: Ohio UP, 1982), 117-18.

17. James Booth, "*Why Are We So Blest?* and the Limits of Metaphor," *Journal of Commonwealth Literature* 4 (1979): 67.

18. Adewale Maja-Pearce, "Just Another Sick Book," review of *Why Are We So Blest?*, by Ayi Kwei Armah, *Okike* 23 (1983): 135-36.

19. Bernth Lindfors, "Armah's Histories," *African Literature Today* 11 (1980): 89.

20. Ibid., 90-91.

21. Ibid., 90.

22. Wole Soyinka, *Myth, Literature and the African World* (Cambridge: Cambridge University Press, 1976), 112.

23. Ibid., 112.

24. Derek Wright, 232.

25. Eustace Palmer, "Negritude Rediscovered: A Reading of the Recent Novels of Armah, Ngugi, and Soyinka," *International Fiction Review* 8, no. 1 (1981): 5.

26. Chinyere Nwahunanya, "A Vision of the Ideal: Armah's *Two Thousand Seasons,*" *Modern Fiction Studies* 37 (autumn 1991): 550.

27. Edward Sackey, "Oral Tradition and the African Novel," *Modern Fiction Studies* 37 (1991): 398.

28. Ibid., 402.

29. Ayi Kwei Armah, *Why Are We So Blest?* (New York: Doubleday, 1973), 222.

30. Derek Wright, 241.

31. Ayi Kwei Armah, "Yaw Manu's Charm," *Atlantic* (May 1968): 89-95.

32. Ayi Kwei Armah, *Why Are We So Blest?*, 231.

33. Norman Albritton Spencer, "Political Consciousness and Commitment in Modern African Literature: A Study of the Novels of Ayi Kwei Armah" (Ph.D diss. State University of New York at Stony Brook, 1985), 232-33.

34. Chinua Achebe, "Africa and Her Writers," in *Morning Yet on Creation Day* (New York: Anchor, 1975), 38.

35. Ibid., 40.

36. Norman A. Spencer, 28.

37. Taban lo Liyong, "Ayi Kwei Armah in Two Moods," *The Journal of Commonwealth Literature* 26 (August 1991): 4.

Chapter 2

The Absurd

According to Alfred Stern, only in those periods of disquiet and uncertainty does the individual feel compelled to question the value and the meaning of his existence. In less catastrophic times, man's being is taken for granted, and he does not question it "because it is as unproblematic and tasteless as the ever-present saliva in our mouths."[1] It is solely the threat of upheaval which forces man to turn inward to seek to re-define himself in relation to the world. Stern writes: "In extreme situations . . . the whole trend of our consciousness is changed. In those extreme situations that we call *crisis,* man asks himself anew the ultimate questions of the meaning, the essence, and the value of human existence."[2] This questioning and the answers it produces Stern associates with existentialism, which he then goes on to define as a *philosophy of crisis.*

Such an extreme situation which prompted the introspection described by Stern was the occupation of France by Nazi forces which alienated the Frenchman from his social milieu by revealing the void upon which all his ideals had been based. Alfred Stern speaks of a "transvaluation of all values" which subverted the ideals of the Third Republic, those of freedom, equality, and justice, into their opposites--those of servitude, violence, and dictatorship--thus resulting in the Frenchman's sense of inertia, alienation and homelessness. As Stern describes the "vacuum of values" created in France during the four years of the German occupation:

> The transvaluation of values in which the young Frenchmen had been educated, created total bewilderment. From one day to the next they heard the negative value of freedom and the positive value of servitude proclaimed, along with the negative value of equality and the positive value of a hierarchy of superior and inferior races, of masters and slaves; as well as the negative value of the idea of a brotherhood of

13

nations and the positive value of treason to an allied nation and one's own nation; the negative value of intelligence and the positive value of instinct; the negative value of law and the positive of violence; the negative value of democracy and the positive of dictatorship; all presented with the quavering voice of a kind old grandfather who wanted to protect his poor immature grandchildren. Those who, on the eve of invasion, had been stigmatized as traitors, were now praised as heroes, while the heroes of yesterday were stigmatized as traitors. The "good" of yesterday became the "evil" of today; the "evil" of yesterday, the "good" of today.[3]

The dereliction of values, described by Stern as characteristic of France both during and following the German occupation, coincides closely with the confusion and anarchy described by Ghanaian author Ayi Kwei Armah as characteristic of Africa during its post-war and post-independence period. Albeit the post-war situation of Africans does not compare in its radicalness to that of Frenchmen held as political captives during the Resistance, the situation described by the Ghanaian author in the novel *The Beautyful Ones Are Not Yet Born* nonetheless sufficiently qualifies as a crisis of values. In the novel, Ayi Kwei Armah speaks of a post-war period marred by irrationality, immorality, and lawlessness. Veteran soldiers returning to their homeland following the Second World War were stunned by the irony at what their engagement abroad had represented: they had sacrificed their lives to protect the freedom of other countries while they, and those left behind, still suffered under the yoke of oppression. The anger at their betrayal found expression in violence, a violence made all the more formidable because they made those closest to them scapegoats for the cruelties visited upon them by the agents of colonialism. As the author speaks of the violence rampant following the war:

> There were the fights, of course, between man and man, not so much over women as over white men asking to be taken to women, and the films brought the intelligent mind clever new fashions in dress and in murder. There were the more exciting, far more complete fights between large groups of violent men, when soldiers for some reason no one cared to know would be fighting policemen, or solid Kroo men would stand and fight the returned warriors. . . . It was also the time of the fashion of the jackknife and the chuke, the rapid unthinking movement of short, ugly iron points that fed wandering living ghosts with what they wanted, blood that would never put an end to their inner suffering.[4]

Some of the post-war disillusionment was linked to the scarcity of jobs. Ex-soldiers who had benefited both from educational and technical training, during the war, returned home to find that their employment opportunities were either limited or non-existent.[5] In the novel, Ayi Kwei Armah speaks of "a hundred men waiting too quietly to fill places enough for seven" (64), and even those who were lucky enough to find work had to satisfy themselves with labor that was "too cruel for white men's hands" (64). Ex-soldier Kofi Billy was "one of the lucky ones." He acquired a job moving cargo at the wharf, but even this was fraught with despair and hardship. One day while Kofi Billy was moving cargo across the deck, a young, inexperienced Englishman overloaded the crane he was operating, and the disengaged steel rope whipped through the air and severed Kofi Billy's right leg. His life thus became afterwards one of inconsolable loss: "He just sat looking at the space which the wood-and-metal limb could never fill, and said nothing" (65).

Many of the veterans attempted to escape the abysmal despair brought on by the war by turning to *wee*. The opiate took the torn victims outside of themselves and allowed them to see the hurtful truths that they purposely had blinded themselves to before. However, because the drug dilated the senses and allowed the users to experience reality with "bodies newly opened up" (70), it was said to be dangerous, and sometimes fatal. Such was ex-soldier Kofi Billy's experience with *wee*. The drug, rather than assuring him of meaning in a world torn by discord, only had the effect of affirming his suspicion of society's purblind impulsion towards destruction. One evening while Kofi Billy and two companions sat smoking *wee* on the beach, he had the vision of so many people like "little bubbles joined together": "They are going, just going, and I am going with them. I know I would like to be able to come out and see where we are going, but in the very long lines of people, I am only one. It is not at all possible to come out and see where we are going. I am just going" (73). After this experience with *wee*, Kofi Billy went into seclusion and later hanged himself.

Suicide, violence and drugs were some of the ways the ex-servicemen found of coping with the spiritual malaise. Another way was petty thievery. The author speaks of a total disconnectedness of loyalties, where people would steal just as easily from friends as they would from strangers. An example of this complete abandonment of traditional values is represented in the fate of Egya Akon.

Egya Akon was a solitary and upright man who lived an ascetic life in the midst of flagrant immorality: "He did not drink or smoke, and did not run after other people's women. . . . He did not have the character to steal from his work" (75-76). Nonetheless, because Egya Akon was perceived as an anomaly, suspicion arose around him. It was rumoured that he hoarded money and immediately became a target for conspirators. One early dawn, he was duped into allowing entrance into his home and was murdered by a band of thieves, led by his trusted friend, Slim Tano. Only negligible amounts of money could have been found, but even this, it was said, was sufficient reason for murder:

A few pounds, maybe, and that was all his killers could have found. But a few pounds then were not things to disappoint men desperate with the disease of the time. We were all discovering something that seemed hard only when it was new. Money was not pieces of paper the farmers burned to show their wealth. Money was life. (76)

Such is the dereliction of values described by Ayi Kwei Armah in the novel that it excludes no one, but extends even to the local marketplace:

Even the women were becoming mean. In the market there was nothing they wanted to give, and they were careful about money in a way that brought the sickness home to all of us. We blamed them, as we blamed ourselves and every other thing that was there to be blamed. What can people do when there remains only so much meaning in their lives and that little meaning is running so irretrievably away with every day that goes? What can people do? We were defending ourselves against our friends as if they were animals. Many things happened then which we ourselves had no way of understanding. (75)

A group of leaders finally emerged to harness the popular unrest and to channel it toward more constructive ends. An official inquiry into the local disturbances had discovered that the underlying cause for the national unrest was the frustration felt by many Africans over their political and economic stagnation.[6] The Second World War had caused a trade boom, creating more jobs and generally improving the financial situation of the country; yet the conditions for the indigenous population remained virtually unchanged. J.D. Fage, in *A History of West Africa: An Introductory Survey,* assesses the post-war situation in West Africa:

The reality of the immediate post-war period was a severe disappointment. The new wealth gained from the high prices for West African produce proved of little value to the average man. The consumer goods he wanted were both expensive and in short supply, and the European importers were suspected of exploiting the situation to their own advantage. For lack of the capital goods required, the new development plans were slow to bring results. While the numbers of their directors, technical advisers, research workers, teachers and the like, brought out from Europe at considerable expense to earn high salaries, continually increased, the opportunities for ambitious Africans who had acquired new educational or technical skills did not.[7]

Spirited agitations, organized strikes, and uncompromising demands for full self-government on the Gold Coast contributed to the bid for national independence. A stronger policy of Africanization was adopted by the British government, and positive steps were taken towards the gradual transfer of authority into the hands of African leaders. Nonetheless, with the advent of national independence, finally won on March 6, 1957, when the Gold Coast was officially renamed Ghana, the lot of the common man underwent little change. He continued to pay

the high costs for foodstuffs and continued to labor under the burden of
high taxes, while his newly-elected leaders squandered money recklessly
and lived lavishly amidst public rumours of fraud and corruption. As
Clyde Chantler, in his book *The Ghana Story,* analyzes the political
climate approximately four years after national independence:

> For some time the country had been seething with rumours of official corruption.
> Ministers and members of the C.P.P. were said to be using their official position for
> personal gain. These rumours were set to rest by the prompt prosecution of two
> ministerial secretaries, the resignation of one of the ministers, and by a commission
> which had been appointed to investigate the allegations. The Prime Minister and
> his colleagues came through the investigations unscathed, but there were many
> people in the country who had doubts about their integrity. [8]

It is against this historical background of social and political
corruption that the plot of *The Beautyful Ones* unfolds. Ayi Kwei
Armah writes of a society so thoroughly corrupt that only two
characters, the anonymous railway clerk designated throughout the novel
as "the man," and Teacher, his friend and confidant, are exempt from
this universal contagion. However, these characters are so battered and
preyed upon that their abstention is itself a source of guilt and shame.
The man is apologetic for his morality, and Teacher retreats into
isolation and apathy rather than fight against what he considers to be a
lost cause. On the other hand, the antithesis to both the man and
Teacher is the Party man Joe Koomson. Koomson stands forth as the
epitome of corruption, but because he is fabulously rich and successful,
he is hailed by society as "a big man" and "a white man" (37). Witness
Oyo's explanation of the overriding philosophy of society and,
indirectly, the reason for Koomson's success. The man reports later to
Teacher:

> "Teacher, my wife explained to me, step by step, that life was like a lot of roads:
> long roads, short roads, wide and narrow, steep and level, all sorts of roads. Next,
> she let me know that human beings were like so many people driving their cars on
> all these roads. This was the point at which she told me that those who wanted to
> get far had to learn to drive fast. And then she asked me what name I would give
> to people who were afraid to drive fast, or to drive at all. I had no name to give
> her, but she had not finished. Accidents would happen, she told me, but the fear of
> accidents would never keep men from driving, and Joe Koomson had learned to
> drive." (57)

Such inversion of conventional standards which turns society on end
is further illustrated in the aping of Western culture by Ghanaians and
the denial of everything that is remotely African. In the novel *The
Beautyful Ones,* Ayi Kwei Armah writes of Ghanaians "trying mightily
to be white" (124). African names are vulgarized in the owners'

attempts to "civilize them." Examples of such unsuccessful attempts at imitation are given as "MILLS-HAYFORD . . . PLANGE-BANNERMAN . . . ATTOH-WHITE . . . KUNTU-BLANKSON" (124-25). The indigenous language of the people is forgotten as Ghanaians adopt such English-sounding expressions as "Jolly good" (124). And decisions are made on matters of dress seemingly independent of climatic considerations. A baby referred to as "black as coal" is described as being confined to a white and pink carriage while simultaneously being stifled in "a lot of woolen finery" (125).

Armah's themes and methods recall Camus's in *The Myth of Sisyphus* and *The Stranger*, and one has good reason to conclude that the existentialist notion of the absurd was a significant influence on Armah. An exploration of the similarities and dissimilarities between the ideas of Armah on the one hand and those of Camus on the other should therefore prove instructive.

In *The Myth of Sisyphus*, a group of essays central to his philosophy, Camus had declared that "there is but one philosophical problem, and that is suicide."[9] Although most readers are led to expect from this shock opening a general treatment of the question of suicide, Camus demonstrates throughout the essay that he is less concerned with re-appraising the sociological and sentimental reasons for suicide than he is with evaluating suicide as a response to the absurd. The act of suicide, because it allows the problem of the absurd to be demonstrated--suicide in itself attests to the utter meaninglessness of existence--offers Camus in *The Myth* an organizational framework for the disclosure of his own absurdist philosophy.

Camus attempts to define the feeling of the absurd by first of all enumerating the various ways the absurd manifests itself. He speaks of a rupture in everyday routine and equates the absurd to man's gradual return to consciousness. For example, an individual may be asked by another what he is thinking, and if his mind is sincerely blank, "that odd state of soul in which the void becomes eloquent, in which the heart vainly seeks the link that will connect it again,"[10] becomes the first sign of the absurd. As well, an individual may be stricken by a moment of lucidity when he discovers his existence to be a gratuitous one: "Rising, streetcar, four hours in the office or the factory, meal, streetcar, four hours of work, meal, sleep, and Monday Tuesday Wednesday Thursday Friday and Saturday according to the same rhythm--this path is easily followed most of the time. But one day the 'why' arises and everything begins in that weariness tinged with amazement."[11]

In addition, a person may live incessantly for the future ("'tomorrow,' 'later on,' 'when you have made your way,' 'you will understand when you are old enough'"), not fully realizing that "after all, it's a matter of dying":

> Yet a day comes when a man notices or says that he is thirty. Thus he asserts his youth. But simultaneously he situates himself in relation to time. He takes his place in it. He admits that he stands at a certain point on a curve that he acknowledges having to travel to its end. He belongs to time, and by the terror that seizes him, he recognizes his worst enemy. Tomorrow, he was longing for tomorrow, whereas everything in him ought to reject it. That revolt of the flesh is the absurd.[12]

Other aspects of the absurd are given as man's discovery that the world is strange, irreducible and therefore not subject to human reason, man's encounter with his face in the mirror and the recognition that it is at once both strange and familiar, and, foremost of all, the supreme absurdity that man faces in death which makes a mockery of all human enterprise. Camus explains:

> If time frightens us, this is because it works out the problem and the solution comes afterward. All the pretty speeches about the soul will have their contrary convincingly proved, at least for a time. From this inert body on which a slap makes no mark the soul has disappeared. This elementary and definitive aspect of the adventure constitutes the absurd feeling. Under the fatal lighting of that destiny, its uselessness becomes evident. No code of ethics and no effort are justifiable *a priori* in the face of the cruel mathematics that command our condition.[13]

Principally, Camus equates the absurd to elements of divorce, struggle and confrontation: "The absurd is essentially a divorce. It lies in neither of the elements compared; it is born of their confrontation."[14] Arguing that to live with the absurd means to give ascendancy to paradox, conflict and chaos, Camus goes on in *The Myth* to consider, historically, the ways man has of dealing with the absurd, disposing of them finally in turn.

In Armah's *The Beautyful Ones*, the same discrepancy and conflict which Camus has described as giving rise to the absurd prevail throughout the novel; however, where death is argued by Camus as the supreme menace which reduces man's hopes to nothingness, Armah uniquely interprets corruption as the nemesis which nullifies man's efforts, thus stripping him of any hopes of triumph.

At the beginning of the novel, Armah is deliberately obscure with regard to fictional setting and locale. As Eldred Jones describes it, "The whole impression is one of Everyman in a field of folk."[15] Despite "the cloak of anonymity," however, the images in the novel point cumulatively to a country whose inhabitants are affected with a spiritual malaise. The people are described as "corpses" and "only bodies walking in their sleep." The hero of the story is referred to conspicuously as "the sleeper," "the watcher," and "the silent one." And the civil servants are depicted as both moving and working in a torpor that is partly the creation of the water from a nearby sea and partly the creation of the men's own silent struggle:

> Sometimes it was possible to taste very clearly the salt that had been eating the walls and the paint on them, if one cared to run one's hand down the dripping surfaces and taste the sticky mess. Partly, too, the wetness came from people, everybody who worked in the office. Everybody seemed to sweat a lot, not from the exertion of their jobs, but from some kind of inner struggle that was always going on. (20)

The cause of the spiritual malaise is the insidious corruption that has invaded the body politic and, by example, has made all moral values appear relative and suspect. This moral disintegration, which paradoxically serves to reward public theft and to condemn honesty as "a very perverse selfishness," epitomizes the absurd and justifies the characters' ultimate feelings of malaise. Two such alienated individuals are the aforementioned characters, the man and Teacher, both of whom are driven to despair because they refuse to become a part of the rat race or to become participants in that country's "national game" of bribery and corruption. For their singular morality, they have to endure the loneliness which results from alienation and to contend with the guilt which accompanies their personal sense of failure. The man feels himself "a criminal" and "the condemned man" because he persists in crawling while "everybody is swimming toward what he wants" (44). His unhappy wife Oyo who dreams of luxury and social betterment ridicules his steadfast morality which prevents him from doing what everybody else is doing, namely, accepting bribes; she labels him an "Onward Christian Soldier" and a "chichidodo bird," a bird that "hates excrement with all its soul" but feeds on maggots which "grow best inside the lavatory" (44).

To further aggravate the man's sense of failure is his harridan of a mother-in-law who looks upon him as both a weakling and a fool and who goes so far as to accuse him of irresponsibility and neglect of his family's well-being. In efforts to goad the man out of his apathy and malaise, she attributes the children's hearty appetites to malnutrition (128-29) and their accidental foot injuries to his own spinelessness (121-22).

Even the innocent chatter of the children remarking the conveniences in the government homes pains the man, since he is once again reminded of the nature of his shortcomings:

> The eyes of the big girl roamed with an unsettled restlessness over everything along the way. Occasionally she was unable to contain some comment about things she

was noticing for the first time, or about people she knew who lived inside the houses they were passing by. The newer houses, middle-type estate houses built by the government for renting, attracted her wonder most. Her comments sounded like words unconnected to anything, . . . but in the adult mind they left an unpleasant echo that turned the child's every perception into the seed of an accusation that would reveal itself with growth. (120)

The man goes to find comfort from his old friend Teacher, but Teacher is worse off because he is completely without hope. Once inspired by the political promise that postdated World War II, Teacher has sunk now into doleful resignation and apathy, having recognized the propensity in society to perpetuate its own delusions. During a visit by the man, Teacher recalls for him the myth of Plato's cave. According to the myth, a group of people had been manacled in chains and, for ages, had been cast into "a deep and cavernous hole." At long last, one is able to break from his chains and to wander into the world of light and colors outside. With eagerness, the wanderer returns to the cave to illuminate those left behind of the pitiable nature of their existence. Those still bound in chains, however, rather than accept the truth of the wanderer's words, instead look upon him as one of those demented:

But to those inside the eternal cave he came as someone driven ill with the breaking of eternal boundaries, and the truth he sought to tell was nothing but the proof of his long delusion, and the words he had to give were the pitiful cries of a madman lost in the mazes of a mind pushed too far out and away from the everlasting way of darkness and reassuring chains. (79).

Teacher, like Plato's bringer of light, feels himself the guardian of those cardinal virtues, prudence, fortitude, temperance and justice; however, unlike Plato's bringer of good, Teacher chooses not to return to the cave, certain that his words will fall upon deaf ears and that those obsessed with the transient and monetary joys of life will carry on their vices without reprieve. This recognition of the unchangeable nature of society now serves as the foundation of his despair. He lives a Spartan existence, lying naked on the bed, devoting his time to reading and listening to "Congo" and "high life" music on the radio. Although he has severed all ties to society, he cannot escape the reach of society. One of the few times Teacher tunes to Radio Ghana, he is confronted with the solitude of his position when a chorus of voices, with all the passion of the multitude they represent, expresses the misery of those who diligently pursue materialistic goals, but who, nevertheless, feel themselves handicapped by society's love of speed:

Those who are blessed with the power
And the soaring swiftness of the eagle
And have flown before,

Let them go.
I will travel slowly,
And I too will arrive. (50)

Kolawole Ogungbesan, in his article "Symbol and Meaning in *The Beautyful Ones Are Not Yet Born,*" contends that the dominant image in the novel is that of a road journey and supports his analogy in part by noting that the novel opens and closes on the road and by calling attention to the speed at which everyone moves. Ogungbesan notes that in general there are three levels of speed which can be identified in the novel. At one extreme are those, like Teacher, who are "metaphorically 'running' from society," and Ogungbesan cites Teacher's lying naked and rigidly immobile on his bed as an example of "this inversion of nature's processes."[16] In the middle is the solitary man who, in Ogungbesan's view, is "the exponent of the 'natural' movement of walking"[17] and who, accordingly, is made heroic because he neither compromises himself for a fraudulent wealth, like Joe Koomson, nor gives himself over completely to despair, like his friend Teacher. According to Ogungbesan:

> The man is heroic because of the doggedness with which he clings to his honesty. His wife thinks he is crawling and wants him to take the leap. Teacher thinks the man is "out there driving" and counsels that he should stand by and watch. He shuns both sides, continues his walk along his honest path, heroically because there is no certainty that he will be proved right.[18]

Counterpoised to the Teacher's extreme position of withdrawal and resignation are "the rich few who are running at top speed." These people are usually seen in their cars, and as Ogungbesan argues, "Their speed is so great that the words 'leap' and 'soar' are used to describe it."[19] An example of those "who are running at top speed" is the extraordinarily rich Joe Koomson. Once a railwayman and dockworker, Koomson has risen now from the ranks of a common labourer to become known as a Party man, and hence "a big man." That Koomson has utilized cunning and craftiness at the expense of the country is immaterial. When the man reminds his wife, who is envious of Estella Koomson, that the Koomsons have acquired their wealth through corrupt means, her remarks reflect typically the blasé attitude of society toward social and political corruption. Their conversation proceeds:

> "Maybe you like this crawling that we do, but I am tired of it. I would like to have someone drive me where I want to go."
> "Like Estella Koomson?"
> "Yes, like Estella. And why not? Is she more than I?"
> "We don't know how she got what she has," the man said.

"And we don't care." The woman's voice had lost its excitement and reverted to its flatness. With a silent gesture she sent the children back inside. "We don't care. Why pretend? Everybody is swimming toward what he wants. Who wants to remain on the beach asking the wind, 'How . . . How . . . How?'" (43-44)

The explanation for all these frantic movements is society's pursuit of "the gleam," a term roughly equated to money, power and influence. As the man describes it: "It is the blinding gleam of beautiful new houses and the shine of powerful new Mercedes cars. It is also the scent of expensive perfumes and the mass of a new wig" (55). Concretized in the structure the Atlantic-Caprice, "the gleam" symbolizes the epitome of wealth and prosperity, but only at the expense of honesty and integrity. For those like the man who are simultaneously attracted and repulsed by "the gleam," it serves as an official mockery of their personal strivings through honest and decent means:

How long would it take, and how hard the work, before there would be enough food for five, and something left over for chasing after the gleam? Only one way. There would always be only one way for the young to reach the gleam. Cutting corners, eating the fruits of fraud. (94)

Because "cutting corners, eating the fruits of fraud" are commonplace practices in what appears to be a money-grubbing society, correspondingly, examples abound of those who, by manner of their pursuit of "the gleam," are drawn into corruption. The infamous Party man Joe Koomson, for example, concocts a boat scheme in order to circumvent government ownership laws which prohibit public officials from owning private property. And as part of the scheme, he arranges for the wife and mother-in-law of the man to become surrogate owners of a fishing boat, to be compensated in return with occasional parcels of fresh fish. Although Koomson's sense of probity may be questioned in this instance, even worse than this ruse to defraud the government is the character's brazenness of attitude which wholly accepts corruption as part of the liberties of political office. When questioned by the mother-in-law as to the source of funds for this all-important venture, Koomson quickly dismisses the question as immaterial, remarking with no small degree of braggadocio: "'The money is not the difficult thing. After all, the Commercial Bank is ours, and we can do anything'" (135).

Moreover, as the novel opens, the conductor of a decrepit and ramshackled bus sits counting the morning's take, regretting that since it is Passion Week and the passengers are living from hand to mouth, he cannot very easily take advantage of them. The conductor's routine check of the coins therefore discloses little if any profit. A second check, however, reveals a cedi note, and the conductor becomes immediately fascinated with the "ancient stale smell" of the note:

> The cedi lay there on the seat. Among the coins it looked strange, and for a moment the conductor thought it was ridiculous that the paper should be so much more important than the shiny metal. In the weak light inside the bus he peered closely at the markings on the note. Then a vague but persistent odor forced itself on him and he rolled the cedi up and deliberately, deeply smelled it. He had to smell it again, this time standing up and away from the public leather of the bus seat. But the smell was not his mistake. Fascinated, he breathed it slowly into his lungs. It was a most unexpected smell for something so new to have: it was a very old smell, very strong, and so very rotten that the stench itself of it came with a curious, satisfying pleasure. (3)

Shame floods the conductor, however, when he notices "a pair of wide-open, staring eyes" at the back of the bus, a pair of eyes he immediately suspects to belong to the giver of the note. He therefore approaches the watcher with the intention of offering him a bribe of cigarettes and, at most, of offering the watcher a share of the day's profit. The shame and fear of the conductor, though, turn quickly into rage and indignation as he discovers that "the watcher" is not a watcher after all, but only a sleeper. He then goes immediately on the offensive: "'You bloodyfucking sonafabitch! Article of no commercial value! You think the bus belongs to your grandfather?'" (5)

Eustace Palmer, in his critical discussion of the novel, views this episode as exemplary of the entire novel and goes on to make the following striking analogy:

> What happens in the bus is a parable of what happens in the country as a whole. The bus, like the State, is in a state of decay, its pieces only held together by rust. The passengers are the ordinary citizens, and the driver and conductor are authority, conniving to defraud the citizens and, if caught, to bribe them into silence.[20]

The analogy Palmer makes, although useful in a general sense, almost falls victim to over-zealousness in criticism. That is, in making a clear-cut distinction between briber and bribee, Palmer runs the risk of isolating corruption and limiting it strictly to political circles. Nonetheless, it is society's *complete* sanction of corruption which makes the morality of the man and Teacher appear so strikingly solitary. Such can be seen in the sheer number of ordinary citizens who, by means of their material pursuits, are drawn into corruption. In chapter seven, the man speaks of Zacharias Lagos, a Nigerian who handsomely profits from his job at the sawmill by selling "great lengths of healthy wood" that he had previously written off. Nonetheless, like Joe Koomson, Lagos, rather than being condemned for theft, is universally cited as a social example. It is noted: "When he was caught people called him a good, generous man, and cursed the jealous man who had informed on him" (95).

Another individual who may be said to have taken the "bold, corrupt leap" toward "the gleam" is Abednego Yamoah. Similar to the Nigerian Zacharias Lagos, Yamoah has been guilty of filching government supplies to sell at personal profit. However, unlike Lagos, Yamoah has never been caught; he is considered therefore a social hero. The man muses:

> Abednego Yamoah, still free, perhaps never to be caught. Selling government petrol for himself, but so cleverly there is always someone else, a messenger, a cleaner, to be jailed, never Abednego. The whole world says he is a good man, and the whole world asks why we are not like him. (95)

Finally, yet another example of the corrupting influence of "the gleam" is represented in the Supervisor of Space Allocations at the Railway and Harbour Administration where the man is employed as clerk. An ousted bursar from "one of the Ghana national secondary schools" (108), the current supervisor had been exposed by the students to the Ministry of Education for financial mis-management; however, like those before him, the bursar had escaped public reprimand and censure. That is, the Ministry had promptly handled the affair by dismissing the students responsible for drafting the letter of complaint, charging them with "gross insubordination" (108), by closing the school in the midst of student uprisings and protests, and by issuing the directive to the Railway Administration to hire the bursar in his present position. And of the supervisor's guilt in the charges leveled against him by the students, there is little doubt. The man reports that in the midst of student rioting, "a fire had gutted the bursar's entire office" (108), undoubtedly set by the allocations clerk who was then in the bursar's employ and who had later been appointed by the supervisor to his present job at the Railway Administration. Here the two continue their corrupt practice of regarding the job as "an opportunity [they] had won for making as much money as [they] could as quickly as [they] could" (108). The man now marvels at the irony of their success: "This place is kind to them, so let the smile. In another country they would be in jail. Here they are heroes" (109).

This complete inversion of social values which congratulates theft and condemns honesty as a social vice accounts then for the extraordinary amount of corruption in Ghanaian society and, concomitantly, for the characters' feelings of malaise and of the absurd. Furthermore, the author, through his concentration on the images of filth, stench, putrefaction and decay, gives the impression that such corruption is inescapable.

As the man descends the bus at the beginning of the novel, he notices the square waste boxes which had served previously as part of a clean-up campaign initiated by the Ministry of Health. The Ministry, announcing that "dirt was undesirable and must be eliminated," had embarked upon an impressive drive to clean up the town by installing "gleaming white" receptacles at strategic points in the city as "shining examples of cleanliness." The receptacles not only were noticed by the folks but were so successful that, ironically, they now serve as examples of the kind of filth they initially were aimed at alleviating. The man notes:

> People used them well, so that it took no time at all for them to get full. People still used them, and they overflowed with banana peels and mango seeds and thoroughly sucked-out oranges and the chaff of sugarcane and most of all the thick brown wrapping from a hundred balls of *kenkey*. People did not have to go up to the boxes any more. From a distance they aimed their rubbish at the growing heap, and a good amount of juicy offal hit the face and sides of the box before finding a final resting place upon the heap. As yet the box was still visible above it all, though the writing upon it could no longer be read. (8)

The irrepressible nature of corruption is again demonstrated in the description of a worn and diseased bannister at the Railway and Harbour Administration where the man is employed at his tedious job as clerk and train dispatcher. The man recalls that "it would be impossible to calculate how much polish on how many rags" the bannister had seen in order to forestall the inevitable decay. However, since "it was in the nature of wood to rot with age," all attempts made by the workers to preserve the wood are acknowledged by the man as both fruitless and inane:

> The wood underneath would win and win till the end of time. Of that there was no doubt possible, only the pain of hope perennially doomed to disappointment. It was so clear. Of course it was in the nature of the wood to rot with age. The polish, it was supposed, would catch the rot. But of course in the end it was the rot which imprisoned everything in its effortless embrace. It did not really have to fight. Being was enough. (12)

Finally, the inevitability of corruption is cogently represented in the character of Rama Krishna. As the man goes to visit Teacher, he recalls his friend Rama Krishna who, sickened by the profuse amount of corruption around him, had turned to Buddhism in a desperate attempt to preserve youth and to achieve immortality. Rama Krishna had plunged himself into yoga and meditative exercises and had given up any diet containing meat. He sustained himself on special diets of honey and vinegar and, in a last-ditch effort to purify himself, had resolved to practice celibacy. This thorough-going attempt by Rama

Krishna to escape corruption, however, in the end, predictably proved fatal. The man recalls that Rama Krishna had died prematurely of consumption and that "where his heart ought to have been there was only a living lot of worms gathered together tightly in the shape of a heart" (48). The man now ponders: "And so what did the dead rot inside the friend not have to do with his fear of what was decaying outside of himself? And what would such an unnatural flight be worth at all, in the end?" (48).

The man's despair finds its echo in Teacher. As Teacher explains the foundation of his pessimism and, consequently, the reason why his words can be of little comfort to his melancholy friend:

> "I don't feel any hope in me any more. I can see things, but I don't feel much. When you can see the end of things even in their beginnings, there's no more hope, unless you want to pretend, or forget. . . . I also am one of the dead people, the walking dead. A ghost. I died long ago. So long ago that not even the old libations of living blood will make me live again." (60)

As already mentioned, the disillusionment of both Teacher and the man is linked to the aftermath of the Second World War. African soldiers recruited to fight during the war returned to their homeland with a sense of betrayal for having fought in an alien war and for having sacrificed their lives for a cause they failed to comprehend. This sense of frustration and betrayal manifested itself in outward violence and in a readiness to follow anyone who offered reason for resurrecting their feelings of hope and optimism. One such nationalist leader was the charismatic Kwame Nkrumah. Distinct from the other Party men and the colonialist hangers-on who barely disguised their greed and avarice and their desire to profit from the political situation, this young leader appealed to believers and skeptics alike through his fervent call for African autonomy and self-sufficiency. The promise that the young Nkrumah offered, however, soon soured as he, like Rama Krishna, proved himself unable to respect the cycle of life which placed limits on youth and sovereignty, and as he likewise succumbed to the lure of wealth and personal affluence. The author notes:

> It was his youth that destroyed him with the powerful ghost of its promise. Had he followed the path traced out by his youth and kept to it, what would have prevented a younger man, one more like himself in the purity of his youth, from coming before him as more fit to keep to the path? A youth who could have lived the way he himself had lived at first, the way he never could have lived again when he became the old man and shiny things began to pull the tired body toward rest and toward decay. . . . Perhaps it is too cruel of us to ask that those approaching the end of the cycle should accept without fear the going and the coming of life and death. (86-87)

Consequently, it is the precipitous rise and fall of the nationalist leader which is at the heart of the novel and which contributes to its tone of despair. The reader is left with the distinct impression that although the existing regime has been finally overturned by a military coup, the corruption that was so much a part of the government will still persist, and that the only noticeable difference is that the capricious reins of government have simply changed hands. As one character surmises: "'Now another group of bellies will be bursting with the country's riches!'" (156).

Ayi Kwei Armah has been called to task for identifying the fictional setting in the latter part of the novel; more specifically, for directing his criticism at the Nkrumah regime. E.N. Obiechina, in his review of the novel, considers "the dragging in of Nkrumah . . . an error in judgment on the part of the novelist" and argues that "the whole thing is capable of stoking up so much unnecessary controversy. The events surrounding Nkrumah's reign and overthrow in Ghana are too complex and open to diverse interpretations to be safely handled in this kind of fiction."[21]

Similarly, Chinua Achebe has considered the identification of an African setting and the inclusion of the Nkrumah reference in the novel "a mistake," concluding that the novel has been unconvincing because "Armah insists that the story is happening in Ghana and not in some modern, existentialist no man's land."[22]

In addition, both Obiechina and Achebe have criticized the motives of the writer, finding, respectively, Armah's scathing denunciations of contemporary Ghanaian society indicative of "neo-colonialism"[23] and of the "alienated writer" bent on selling his wares to European audiences. On the latter charge, Achebe has written:

> Ayi Kwei Armah is the alienated native. It seems that to achieve the modern alienated stance an African writer will end up writing like some white District Officer.
> Armah is quoted somewhere as saying that he is not an African writer but just a writer. Some other writers (and friends of mine, all) have said the same thing. It is a sentiment guaranteed to win applause in Western circles. But it is a statement of defeat. A man is never more defeated than when he is running away from himself.[24]

Although it may be granted the superfluousness of the Nkrumah reference, given the parabolic nature of the literature, the *ad hominem* attacks in the charges by Obiechina and Achebe make their criticism suspect. To devaluate the literature based upon what the critic perceives as artistic flaws is one thing; but to devaluate the literature by calling into question the integrity of the author is quite another. The latter not only openly discounts a sense of fair play by threatening to reduce criticism to mudslinging, but likewise serves to cloud the issue by making the author, not the literature, the primary focus of attention. Inherent in the remarks by Obiechina and Achebe is therefore yet another reason for the rejection of the nationalistic criticism as proposed by Irele, since their remarks reveal, respectively, the dangers of making the socio-political views of the author, not necessarily the writer's fictional dramatization of those views, the primary standard of judgement. As Robert Fraser has noted in his work *The Novels of Ayi Kwei Armah*, behind the remarks by Obiechina is a barely-disguised subjectivism which, in its irrelevance, becomes both a disservice to the author and, by extension, to the body of African criticism. He has written:

> E.N. Obiechina talks of its *[The Beautyful Ones']* "rigid moral positions"; Molly Mahood concludes that "the dominating mood of the novel is one of almost total disillusionment." Behind many of these opinions one can discern the shadow of a defensive posture. Confronted with a work so destructive of patriotic complacency, many critics have tended to confuse the charge of treason with that of artistic deficiency. Hence Armah comes to be saddled with strictures which are essentially political rather than artistic in nature. His misfortune in this regard is similar to another writer from the Third World; the Trinidadian novelist, V.S. Naipaul. In both, a determination to see things straight has been taken as a kind of obsessive and twisted acidity. The charge is distinctly unfair to both of them.[25]

These reservations of Obiechina's review of the novel notwithstanding, Obiechina makes a valid point regarding the hasty stereotyping of politicians in the novel. Nkrumah and the Party men emerge almost overwhelmingly in the novel as ruffians, an image completely inconsistent with historical accounts which extol Nkrumah's "determination and understanding of political organization," as well as "an honest belief in his cause."[26] At the same time, however, political and social historians are not remiss in criticizing the leader's mismanagement of governmental funds and exploitation of political office, thereby giving credence to Armah's observations on the nationalist leader's corrupt politics. Clyde Chantler, for example, sees Nkrumah's rise to power as "perhaps the beginning of the classic story of the dictator which power corrupted; the beginning of the change in his personality from the man who lived like the masses, to the rich and powerful leader who enjoyed a life of luxury."[27] P.C. Lloyd is in virtual agreement when he cites the politicians' "ostentatious luxury" as the primary cause of disillusionment among Ghanaian constituency, an ostentatiousness which, despite Nkrumah's pleas for austerity, went continually unchecked. Lloyd writes:

> In his 1961 Dawn Broadcast, which served to herald a more puritanical era, Nkrumah ruled that party members should not own more than two houses with a combined value of £20,000 or more than two cars. Such limits seem significantly

generous for men whose previous careers, often as teachers or clerks, would have earned them salaries below £500 a year. Initially, people accepted the affluence of their elected representatives, feeling that it symbolized not only his own success but also the dignity of his constituency; it was merited by the benefits which he attracted for his people. But as the benefits cease to flow, and the representative grows wealthier and more remote from his constituents, these people do not forget that he owes his position to their votes. They may flatter him when they seek favours, but the general attitude becomes one of disillusion. [28]

Finally, a corroboration of these assertions is contained in Martin Meredith's article "The Broken Dream," wherein Meredith notes that the free-spending of Nkrumah and the party elite effectively morgaged Ghana's future: "At independence, Ghana, one of the richest countries in the world, had reserves of about £200 million. Toward the end of Nkrumah's rule, nine years later, the reserves were down to £30 million, and debts stood at £360 million."[29] The obscene spending associated with the Nkrumah era is documented in the report provided by Meredith of "the wife of one minister [acquiring] a £3000 gold-plated bed from a London store, until a well-publicised scandal forced her to send it back."[30]

The "obscene haste" of Nkrumah's fall into corruption is effectively encapsulated in the image of the manchild described in chapter six of *The Beautyful Ones.* Described as born with all the features of a human baby, this human oddity, in seven years, had completed "the cycle from babyhood to infancy to youth, to maturity and old age, and in its seventh year it had died a natural death." Its grotesqueness now stems from the marked incongruity between its lifespan and its outward demeanor:

> The manchild looked more irretrievably old, far more thoroughly decayed, than any ordinary old man could ever have looked. But of course, it, too, had a nature of its own, so that only those who have found some solid ground they can call the natural will feel free to call it unnatural. (62)

This dizzying speed of decay and corruption, brought on by the Africans' desire to become "the dark ghost of a European" or to supplant their "white masters" in the exploitation of the African people, becomes then the object of criticism in *The Beautyful Ones.*

Attending the author's criticism of the materialist retrogression of the body polity is also his criticism of the dissolution, within society at large, of traditionally-held convictions and beliefs. A recurring comment in the novel is "'but he was my classmate.'" The man has difficulty accepting the success of Koomson, given his rather commonplace background. Now his former schoolmate, a past dockworker, has the elaborate title of "His Excellency Joseph Koomson,

Minister Plenipotentiary, Member of the Presidential Commission, Hero of Socialist Labor" (55).

Hence, it is the corruption of traditional communal standards or, more specifically, the complete inversion of traditional morality which introduces feelings of distress and doubt and which leads ultimately to the man's severe apathy and malaise. As he confides in Teacher: "I am asking myself what is wrong with me. Do I have some part missing? Teacher, this Koomson was my own classmate. . . . So tell me, what is wrong with me?'" (56).

In some respects, the respective responses of tortured passivity and resignation by the man and Teacher are at variance with the spirit of the absurd, at least according to its definition by Camus. For example, in *The Myth of Sisyphus* Camus had rejected out of hand total despair, suicide and hope as legitimate responses to the absurd, since they either involved resignation or psychological deceit. The only fitting alternative he saw to man's absurd condition was either to live aggressively or to revolt against what he considered the meaninglessness of life:

> Living is keeping the absurd alive. Keeping it alive is, above all, contemplating it. Unlike Eurydice, the absurd dies only when we turn away from it. One of the most coherent philosophical positions is thus revolt. It is a constant confrontation between man and his own obscurity. It is an insistence upon an impossible transparency. It challenges the world anew every second. Just as danger provided man the unique opportunity of seizing awareness, so metaphysical revolt extends awareness to the whole of experience. It is that presence of man in his own eyes. It is not aspiration, for it is devoid of hope. That revolt is the certainty of a crushing fate, without the resignation that ought to accompany it.[31]

The absurd man, as Camus describes him, is therefore free of the illusions that either faith or concern for the future offers. Aware that death destroys all plans and reduces them to nothingness, the absurd man is determined to accumulate a range of sensual experiences in defiance of death. Camus lists as examples of the absurd hero Don Juan, the actor, the adventurer and the artist. What these heroes share in common is a passion for life, a lack of regret for the past and an indifference for the future. The notorious love Don Juan, for example, does not quest after eternal love. Instead he practices a love which "recognizes itself to be both short-lived and exceptional."[32] The actor is similarly immersed in the moment. Like Don Juan, he subscribes to the ethics of quantity and expends himself for the re-creation of a few ephemeral moments on stage.

The character, though, who best epitomizes the absurd hero is the myth character Sisyphus. "His scorn of the gods, his hatred of death, and his passion for life" earned him the insuperable task of rolling a boulder up a steep slope, only to have it descend again once he had reached the summit. However, because Sisyphus retains consciousness, he "knows the whole extent of his wretched condition," he is remarkably able to transcend his fate and, at the same time, to salvage his pride and dignity:

> If this myth is vague, that is because its hero is conscious. Where would his torture be, indeed, if at every step the hope of succeeding upheld him? . . . Sisyphus, proletarian of the gods, powerless and rebellious, knows the whole extent of his wretched condition: it is what he thinks of during his descent. The lucidity that was to constitute his torture at the same time crowns his victory. There is no fate that cannot be surmounted by scorn.[33]

The classic example of Camus's philosophy of revolt is exemplified in *The Stranger*, who exhibits the fundamental traits attributed to the absurd hero in *The Myth of Sisyphus*, namely a passion for life, a desire for truth, and conscious revolt against the inevitable fate of death. In *The Myth of Sisyphus* Camus had maintained that one of the consequences of lucidity was unbridled freedom. Before encountering the absurd, man was enslaved by his fidelity to principles, presumptions and prejudices. Envisioning a life based upon purpose and direction, man immersed himself in expectations and desires which subsequently robbed him of his freedom: "Thus I could not act otherwise than as the father (or the engineer or the leader of a nation, or the post-office subclerk) that I am preparing to be."[34] After encountering the absurd, however, the question of principles and values became moot, since "death is there as the only reality."[35] The absurd individual, recognizing that for him there was no future, therefore freed himself unconditionally "to use everything that is given" within the bounds of a limited fate:

> If I admit that my freedom has no meaning except in relation to its limited fate, then I must say that what counts is not the best living but the most living. It is not up to me to wonder if this is vulgar or revolting, elegant or deplorable. Once and for all, value judgments are discarded here in favor of factual judgments. I have merely to draw the conclusions from what I can see and to risk nothing that is hypothetical. Supposing that living in this way were not honorable, then true propriety would command me to be dishonorable.[36]

In *The Stranger*, as in *The Myth*, a quantitative ethic is similarly observed. This is to say that, quite opposed to the presumptions entertained by others in the novel, Meursault lives only for the moment, for the fulfillment of present sensation. At the Home for Aged Persons, little if any detail escapes the dispassionate notice of the character. He observes meticulously the features and the articles of clothing of the elderly inmates, feels somewhat inconvenienced by the death of his mother ("I hadn't been in the country for ages, and I caught myself thinking what an agreeable walk I could have had, if it hadn't been for Mother"),[37] and, following the burial ceremony, can only recall the red geraniums atop the graves, the color of the earth, and the white roots mixed with the soil covering his mother's coffin. Albert Maquet, in fact, in the critical work *Albert Camus: An Invincible Summer,* sees a distinct correlation between the character's preoccupation with external phenomena and his general lack of emotion. He explains:

> To experience a feeling presupposes continuity. . . . The "It's all the same to me" that constantly returns to his [Meursault's] lips is understandable. In order to express a judgment of value, it is necessary to base oneself on memory or have an imagination as to the future. In the flow of the present, all hierarchy is void of meaning.[38]

Aside from the absurd reality that Meursault also commits murder under the influence of external sensation--he is temporarily blinded by the sun and approaches the Arab, aware that such action could precipitate a brutal confrontation--the greatest manifestation of the absurd nonetheless occurs at the conclusion of the novel. There Meursault, facing execution for murder, successfully re-affirms the themes(s) expounded upon in *The Myth,* namely, the theme of revolt in response to the absurd. Heretofore, Meursault had been wholly accepting of the mechanical existence which essentially robbed him of his humanity. Nonetheless, faced with the immanence of death, Meursault finally awakens from his somnambulism to discover the limits placed on life and the greater need to savor life, even as one is on the brink of annihilation. In words reminiscent of *The Myth,* Meursault defiantly expresses the absolute purposelessness of life:

> I'd been right, I was still right, I was always right. I'd passed my life in a certain way, and I might have passed it in a different way, if I'd felt like it. I'd acted thus, and I hadn't acted otherwise; I hadn't done *x,* whereas I had done *y* or *z.* And what did that mean? That, all the time, I'd been waiting for this present moment, for that dawn, tomorrow's or another day's, which was to justify me. Nothing, nothing had the least importance, and I knew quite well why.[39]

It is at this moment of lucidity that consciousness is re-awakened, and Meursault realizes the ideal conception of the absurd hero. For the first time in months, he remembers his mother and is sympathetic of her desire to take a fiancé so late in life. Like her as well, he recognizes the value and the worth of life, perhaps now even more so because of its recognized superfluousness:

I, too, felt ready to start life all over again.   It was as if that great rush of anger had washed me clean, emptied me of hope, and, gazing up at the dark sky spangled with its signs and stars, for the first time, the first, I laid my heart open to the benign indifference of the universe. To feel it so like myself, indeed, so brotherly, made me realize that I'd been happy, and that I was happy still. For all to be accomplished, for me to feel less lonely, all that remained to hope was that on the day of my execution there should be a huge crowd of spectators and that they should greet me with howls of execration.[40]

Compared to Camus's theory of dialectical revolt which, according to Thomas Hanna, "is as positive as it is negative, it affirms as much as it denies, it says Yes to something within man that is irreducible, and it says No to something outside man which is unacceptable,"[41] it may be argued that Armah's conciliatory attitude in *The Beautyful Ones* amounts to escapism. Margaret Folarin, in the article "An Additional Comment on Ayi Kwei Armah's *The Beautyful Ones Are Not Yet Born,"* has already identified the recurring images of salt and salt water which, she argues, dilute the metaphors of despair and account ultimately for the prevailing elements of faith and promise in the novel. She notes particularly chapter six where Maanan, a prostitute, Kofi Billy, an ex-soldier, and Teacher sit smoking *wee* on the beach. Teacher is made suddenly aware of Maanan for the first time, not as woman as body, but as an embodiment of suffering womanhood. Concurrently, Teacher is made aware of his own impotence to sustain and complement her rare essence and reaches out a searching hand placatingly to her. Ironically though he gathers only "a handful of fine, beautiful sand, and the beauty of the sand" takes his gaze away from "the troubled beauty of the woman" beside him:

> I could not help it as the moist sand dripped through my weakened fingers and joined the shore. Like an animal I knelt down and stretched out my hand to wash the sand away with the farthest coming water of the waves, and then suddenly I felt like taking the salt water into my mouth. It was not only salt I tasted, but a hundred other strong things in the water, and I cleansed my mouth with it and spat it out slowly and did it again. Something that did not want to die made me touch Maanan softly on the side of her mouth. For a long time my hand rested there and I looked at her and I was lost in despair. (72)

Folarin speaks of the images of salt and salt water in the paragraph as representing the cycle of life: "Salt, like the sea, is the destroyer and it is also the preserver of living things, an instrument of decay and of cleansing.   Salt water contains traces of life in its beginnings and endings."[42] She uses this analogy in part to justify her conclusion that the novel is "a bold and cleansing one" and that despite the pessimism, the final values that emerge from the book are not negative ones: "It [the novel] begins with a refusal to accept any sentimental facts about human nature or the social scene. It accepts life as it may be observed at its very worst and still unravels, if in a rather humourless way, much of the value of human existence."[43]

Although other critics may feel compelled to go looking for strawmen in the literature in order to support the charge of morbidity on the part of the author, Folarin's observation nonetheless is well-founded inasmuch as it takes as its cue the notion implicit in the title--that although "the beautiful ones" are not yet born, hope still remains that a rebirth is possible. However, for Camus who has written in *The Myth of Sisyphus* that "knowing whether or not one can live *without appeal* is all that interests me,"[44] the attitude of hope as adopted by Armah is the equivalent of philosophical evasion, since it violates the terms of the equation, unceasing struggle and confrontation, thus destroying altogether the principle of the absurd:

> Everything that destroys, conjures away, or exorcises these requirements (a total absence of hope, a continual rejection, and a conscious dissatisfaction) ruins the absurd and devaluates the attitude that may then be proposed. The absurd has meaning only in so far as it is not agreed to.[45]

In addition to what Camus would call "a leap of faith," or "the mind's retreat before what the mind itself has brought to life"[46] (the absence of revolt), the two writers also differ in their presentation of the absurd. For example, in *The Beautiful Ones* Armah utilizes satire to underscore the insidious social and political corruption, while Albert Camus chooses an ambiguous tone complementary to the lack of order and meaning he finds in the universe. The difference in fact can be seen in juxtaposing the language and tone of *The Stranger* to those of *The Beautyful Ones Are Not Yet Born*. For example, as Sartre has maintained in the article "An Explication of *The Stranger*," in congruence with Camus's theory of absurd art in *The Myth*, *The Stranger* is completely devoid of moral message: "It does not come out of a 'satisfied' kind of thinking, intent on furnishing formal proofs."[47] Instead, Camus borrows the journalistic style of Ernest Hemingway, of reconstituting human experience without bothering at all to apply it to causality. Conjunctive terms such as "because," "therefore," and "hence" are avoided and are replaced rather by terms which evoke either disjunction or mere addition. Such can be seen in the following passage which discourages any theory of explanation and order other than that of pure succession:

> A moment later she asked me if I loved her. *I said that sort of question had no meaning, really; but I supposed I didn't. She looked sad for a bit,* but when we were getting our lunch ready she brightened up and started laughing, and when she

laughs I always want to kiss her. It was just then that the row started in Raymond's room. (Italics mine.)[48]

Leo Pollmann, in the critical work *Sartre and Camus*, had spoken similarly about a "horizontality" or unrelatedness of expression; that is, structural continuity is avoided. Instead, with each new sentence, reality is dissolved and is successively reborn. With reference to the Stranger himself, Pollmann had noted:

> The Stranger is certainly not soulless; he is merely absolutely horizontal. Everything structured, every kind of connection, is alien to him. He is--and here he is a perfect though unintentional illustration of what Sartre regards as existentiality-- immediacy of action created anew from moment to moment.[49]

In *The Myth*, Camus had corroborated views introduced by Sartre and Pollmann when he referred to creation as "the great mime" and noted that "describing . . . is the last ambition of an absurd thought."[50] In Camus's view, the artist's attempt to explain was deemed superfluous, since the provenience of literature was interwoven with the artist's contemplation of the very paradoxes which favor the absurd. In Camus's words, "If the world were clear, art would not exist."[51]

On the other hand, a far cry from the humility of Camus, which conceives of all literature as gratuitous, is the grandiloquent style and manner of Ayi Kwei Armah, especially in the novel *The Beautiful Ones Are Not Yet Born*. For example, unlike Camus, who feels that the desire to judge and to reason experience is a "pretension to the eternal,"[52] Armah in *The Beautiful Ones* assumes such a moral tone that it interferes with the fictional realism and authenticity he hopes to achieve. An example is the description of the Party man Koomson, whose presentation clearly smacks of authorial intervention:

> His mouth had the rich stench of rotten menstrual blood. The man held his breath until the new smell had gone down in the mixture with the liquid atmosphere of the Party man's farts filling the room. At the same time Koomson's insides gave a growl longer than usual, an inner fart of personal, corrupt thunder which in its fullness sounded as if it had rolled down all the way from the eating throat thundering through the belly and the guts, to end in further silent pollution of the air already thick with flatulent fear. (161)

This subordination of fictional reality to theme becomes therefore one of the primary targets of criticism by reviewers of the novel. Eustace Palmer, for instance, identifies the characters in the novel as "types, or symbolic figures, who do not seem to have transcended their theoretical conceptions" and goes on to comment:

It is a pity that in a novel about corruption, Armah has not put them in interesting situations in which corruption is demonstrated. Instead, he has chosen to rely on his (admittedly powerful) exploitation of certain symbols. Perhaps the criticism of this novel relates to moral fables in general. In the moral fable the message is, of necessity, insistent, since almost every other aspect of the novel has to be subordinated to the message.[53]

The two writers, when considered in terms of authorial tone and language, may be said, therefore, to differ remarkably in their responses to the absurd. Whereas Camus in *The Stranger* illuminates a view of the world dominated by divorce and disorientation, Ayi Kwei Armah, contrastingly, by entertaining a coherent vision of the world compatible with traditional values and beliefs, maintains his hold on faith and conventional authority, thus dissolving the tension and contrast which had given rise to the absurd. As Camus hade noted in *The Myth:*

Living an experience, a particular fate, is accepting it fully. Now, no one will live this fate, knowing it to be absurd, unless he does everything to keep before him that absurd brought to light by consciousness. Negating one of the terms of the opposition on which he lives amounts to escaping it. To abolish conscious revolt is to elude the problem.[54]

Nonetheless, despite the discrepancy between the two writers, which may be looked upon as faith on the one hand versus revolt on the other, the two writers do share the *self-same language of the absurd.* That is, the disparity between man's appetite for understanding and the impenetrability of the world, which gives rise to the sentiment of the absurd in Camus's *The Myth of Sisyphus* and *The Stranger,* likewise accounts for the sense of the absurd in Armah's *The Beautyful Ones.*

Another point of comparison is the writers' description of the monotonousness of daily life which gradually leads the individual to the consciousness of the meaninglessness of life. The man in *The Beautyful Ones* discovers that one of the senior clerks at the Railway and Harbour Administration, in order to fill the regular hours of a working day, had invented an elaborate scheme of filing which stretched a mere thirty minutes of work over an entire eight-hour day. The man describes a regimen which consisted of

Alphabetical listings that would never serve any purpose; a search to try and find on the postmark the exact minute every letter was supposed to have been mailed; three transfers of all the lists to cleaner paper, each time in more careful, more beautiful lettering, with not a single smudge: periodic visits to the lavatory, from habit, not necessity. (154)

Correspondingly, in Camus's novel *The Stranger,* a typical Sunday in the life of the character is described:

> After lunch, I felt at loose ends and roamed about the little flat. It suited us well enough when Mother was with me, but now that I was by myself it was too large and I'd moved the dining table into my bedroom. That was now the only room I used; it had all the furniture I needed: a brass bedstead, a dressing table, some cane chairs whose seats had more or less caved in, a wardrobe with a tarnished mirror. The rest of the flat was never used, so I didn't trouble to look after it.
> A bit later, for want of anything better to do, I picked up an old newspaper that was lying on the floor and read it. There was an advertisement of Kruschen Salts and I cut it out and pasted it into the album where I keep things that amuse me in the papers. Then I washed my hands and, as a last resource, went out on the balcony.[55]

The feelings of lethargy and entrapment for both characters are linked to the idealism of a lost youth. From the Stranger's own admission, it is learned that he was not always wanting in ambition. As a student, he had experienced both spur and incentive. But when forced to end prematurely his studies, he soon recognized the pointlessness of his diligence: "As a student I'd had plenty of ambition. . . . But, when I had to drop my studies, I very soon realized all that was pretty futile."[56]

Although the reader is not given the exact reason for the abrupt termination of the Stranger's studies, it is specifically noted in *The Beautyful Ones* that the unexpected pregnancy of the man's soon-to-be wife hastened his attention to practical matters which later gained ascendancy over all other concerns: "It looked as if the important thing was simply that he had cut himself off from the future, that he had chosen to make the dry struggles of the present stretch out and consume the whole of his life to come" (117).

In conclusion, it may be said that both authors treat the alienation and déracination of the individual which have grown out of the negative experiences of a national phenomenon. For Camus, this sense of cosmic despair was part of the disenfranchisement felt by the Frenchmen, following World War II and the period of the Resistance, which called into question the Renaissance values of progress, stability and a sense of oneness with the universe, while for Ayi Kwei Armah, this feeling of divorce was associated with the disillusionment felt by many Ghanaians, following their nation's independence, over the corruptibility of their leaders and the apparent dissolution and abandonment of traditional values. Notwithstanding that the social and political environment which affected their intellectual outlook remained distinct for each writer, irrespective of the source of their disillusionment, each writer, in his own way, has successfully broken through the social veneer of his society in order to reveal the absurd, and likewise the tragic, predicament of modern man.

1. Alfred Stern, *Sartre: His Philosophy and Existential Psychoanalysis*, 2nd ed., rev. and enl. (New York: Delacorte Press, 1967), 104.

2. Ibid., 104.

3. Ibid., 111.

4. Ayi Kwei Armah, *The Beautyful Ones Are Not Yet Born* (New York: Houghton Mifflin, 1968), 65. All subsequent references to this edition will appear in the text.

5. J.D. Fage, *A History of West Africa: An Introductory Survey*, 4th ed. (Cambridge: Cambridge UP, 1969), 208.

6. Ibid., 209.

7. Ibid., 208.

8. Clyde Chantler, *The Ghana Story* (London: Linden Press, 1971), 139.

9. Albert Camus, *The Myth of Sisyphus and Other Essays*, trans. Justin O'Brien (New York: Alfred A. Knopf, 1955), 3.

10. Ibid., 12.

11. Ibid., 12-13.

12. Ibid., 13-14.

13. Ibid., 15-16.

14. Ibid., 30.

15. Eldred Jones, review of *The Beautyful Ones Are Not Yet Born*, by Ayi Kwei Armah, in *African Literature Today: Journal of Explanatory Criticism* 3 (1969): 55.

16. Kolawole Ogungbesan, "Symbol and Meaning in *The Beautyful Ones Are Not Yet Born*," *African Literature Today* 7 (1975): 94.

17. Ibid., 105.

18. Ibid., 106.

19. Ibid., 94-95.

20. Eustace Palmer, *An Introduction to the African Novel: A Critical Study of Twelve Books* (New York: Africana Publishing Corporation, 1972), 131.

21. E.N. Obiechina, review of *The Beautyful Ones Are Not Yet Born*, by Ayi Kwei Armah, in *Okike: A Nigerian Journal of New Writing* 1 (April 1971): 52.

22. Chinua Achebe, *Morning Yet on Creation Day* (New York: Anchor/Doubleday Press, 1975), 39.

23. Obiechina, 52-53.

24. Achebe, *Morning Yet on Creation Day*, 41-42.

25. Robert Fraser, *The Novels of Ayi Kwei Armah* (London: Heinemann, 1980), 15.

26. Chantler, 129, 127.

27. Ibid., 132.

28. P.C. Lloyd, *Africa in Social Change: West African Societies in Transition* (New York: Frederick A. Praeger, 1968), 312.

29. Martin Meredith, "The Shattered Dream: The Sorry State of Ghana, 25 Years After the High Hopes of Independence," *The Sunday Times Magazine*, 7 March 1982, 31.

30. Ibid., 31.

31. Camus, *The Myth*, 54.

32. Ibid., 74.

33. Ibid., 121.

34. Ibid., 58.

35. Ibid., 57.

36. Ibid., 60-61.

37. Albert Camus, *The Stranger*, trans. Stuart Gilbert (New York: Alfred A. Knopf, 1946), 14.

38. Albert Maquet, *Albert Camus: The Invincible Summer* (New York: George Braziller, 1958), 54.

39. Camus, *The Stranger*, 151-52.

40. Ibid., 154.

41. Thomas Hanna, "Albert Camus: Man in Revolt," in *Existential Philosophers: Kierkegaard to Merleau-Ponty*, ed. George Schraeder (New York: McGraw-Hill, 1967), 340-41.

42. Margaret Folarin, "An Additional Comment on Ayi Kwei Armah's *The Beautyful Ones Are Not Yet Born*," *African Literature Today* 5 (1971): 123.

43. Ibid., 128.

44. Camus, *The Myth*, 60.

45. Ibid., 31.

46. Ibid., 50.

47. Jean-Paul Sartre, "An Explication of *The Stranger*." In *Camus: A Collection of Critical Essays*, ed. Germaine Brée (Englewood Cliffs, N.J.: Prentice-Hall, 1962), 111.

48. Camus, *The Stranger*, 44.

49. Leo Pollmann, *Sartre and Camus: Literature of Existence* (New York: Frederick Ungar, 1970), 133.

50. Camus, *The Myth*, 94.

51. Ibid., 98.

52. Ibid., 98.

53. Palmer, *An Introduction to the African Novel*, 142.

54. Camus, *The Myth*, 53-54.

55. Camus, *The Stranger*, 25-26.

56. Ibid., 52.

Chapter 3

The Other

In Jean-Paul Sartre's short story "The Room," Eve is married to Pierre who is afflicted with a mental disorder. The symptoms of his disease include hallucinations, amnesia and paranoia. He hallucinates about statues that "fly around and make fishy eyes at him," constructs a zuithre out of cardboard in a desperate attempt "to conjure the statues," refers to his wife, Eve, as "Agatha," and accuses both his father-in-law and his wife of plotting against him. However, after three years of marriage, Eve remains devoted to her husband. She refuses to have him institutionalized although it has already been medically determined that in another three years, he will sink into complete dementia. Instead, she now leads a life of isolation and loneliness, shunning the outside world and attempting to enter the mad universe of her husband. Alone with Pierre, Eve almost succeeds in believing that the two of them can "live solely by imagination." It is only when her father invades their privacy and begins to treat Pierre as the mad man that he is that Eve becomes aware of Pierre as one of the handicapped, and experiences shame before the Other. This shame justifies Eve's feelings of resentment towards her father, which is manifested following one of his routine weekly visits:

> She twisted her hands around the back of the armchair: she had just remembered her father's eyes. M. Darbedat was bent over Pierre with a competent air; he had said "That's good!" the way someone says when they speak to invalids. He had looked and Pierre's face had been painted in the depths of his sharp bulging eyes. *I hate him when he looks at him because I think he sees him.*[1]

"The Room" captures succinctly what Sartre has treated in *Being and Nothingness* as the justification for both the failure of love and for man's original fall. As he explains it, self-consciousness is brought about only through *the Look* and the judgement of the Other. Without

the Other, a person remains the fullness of his possibilities; he remains a 'for-itself', a term which Sartre equates to the human subjectivity which is a vast nothingness never coincident with itself. Without the Other, there is no transcendent view to confer judgement or value on any given act. Man is completely the sum of his acts, and there is no "outside" against which he can be measured or against which he can evaluate himself.

To illustrate the non-reflective nature of our conscious lives, Sartre gives us the example of the man who, out of jealousy or curiosity, listens through a keyhole. The door and the keyhole posit themselves as instruments to be employed toward the attainment of a certain goal. "They are presented as 'to be handled with care;' the keyhole is given as 'to be looked through close by and a little to one side,' etc. Hence from this moment 'I do what I have to do.'"[2] The man is without a reflective awareness, since his acts and his consciousness are both one and the same: "My consciousness sticks to my acts, it is my acts; and my acts are commanded only by the ends to be attained and by the instruments to be employed."[3] The man cannot be defined, since he constantly transcends himself toward new possibilities. It is only when the man perceives himself as being the object of another's gaze, i.e., the man hears footsteps and becomes aware of an intruder who observes him, that freedom escapes him and becomes commensurate with the freedom of another. This condition of "being looked at" Sartre therefore compares to a hemorrhage where "the flight is without limit," since the individual is captured in still life and is given a definition over which he has absolutely no control: "The world flows out of the world and I flow outside myself. The Other's look makes me be beyond my being in this world and puts me in the midst of the world which is at once *this world* and beyond this world."[4]

The modality of being which is characteristically inert, passive, and closed within itself, Sartre classifies in *Being and Nothingness* as the 'being in-itself'. The 'being in-itself' Sartre distinguishes from its opposite, the 'being for-itself', by the very nature of its absoluteness. Whereas the 'being for-itself' is always a projection outward toward future possibilities, the 'being in-itself', on the other hand, is described as an invariable which is complete unto itself: "being in-itself is what it is. . . . The latter in fact . . . has to be what it is."[5] Because the 'being in-itself' needs no exterior forces in order to be, i.e., it is irreducible, unassailable, gelatinous in its utter contingency, it is looked upon as *de trop*, ugly, insulting, even obscene. This confrontation with the gratuitous nature of the 'being in-itself' is the source of Roquentin's despair in *Nausea:*

In the way: it was the only relationship I could establish between these trees, these gates, these stones. In vain I tried to *count* the chestnut trees, to *locate* them by their relationship to the Velleda, to compare their height with the height of the plane trees: each of them escaped the relationship in which I tried to enclose it, isolated itself, and overflowed. Of these relations (which I insisted on maintaining in order to delay the crumbling of the human world, measures, quantities, and directions)--I felt myself to be the arbitrator; they no longer had their teeth into things. *In the way,* the chestnut tree there, opposite me, a little to the left. *In the way,* the Velleda. . . .[6]

Although the 'being in-itself' is ascribed to the world of inanimate objects, a person too can become thing-like under the gaze of the Other. When a look is cast by the Other, self-hood or freedom of action is denied as one becomes immediately transformed into an object, into a thing-to-be-looked-at: "For the Other, I am a coward, a hypocrite, or just lazy; or, if one prefers, honest and generous--just as the table is a table and the inkwell is an inkwell."[7] Because *the Look* of the Other invariably succeeds in petrifying our freedom and in making us aware of our vulnerability or of our nakedness in the world, Sartre, in *Being and Nothingness,* likens the Other's presence in the world to man's original sin; the alienation experienced by *the Look* of the Other to man's original fall:

My original fall is the existence of the Other. Shame--like pride--is the apprehension of myself as a nature although that very nature escapes me and is unknowable as such. Strictly speaking, it is not that I perceive myself losing my freedom in order to become a *thing,* but my nature is--over there, outside my lived freedom--as a given attribute of this being which I am for the Other.[8]

It is doubtful whether Ayi Kwei Armah, in writing *The Beautyful Ones Are Not Yet Born* and *Fragments,* had the self-same ideas as had Sartre in the short story "The Room" and in the subsequent works *Being and Nothingness* and *No Exit,* where Sartre accused the Other as being the natural foe and stumbling block to man's personal freedom; nonetheless, as congruent with Sartre's estimation of the Other in these foregoing works, Armah, in *The Beautyful Ones* and *Fragments,* likewise attributes the anguish, shame, and guilt felt by the characters to the uncompromising look and judgement of the Other.

It must be pointed out, however, that by *the Look* Sartre gives the reader to understand that he has more in mind than a reference to the eye as "a sensible organ of vision." Although *the Look* most often is "the convergence of two ocular globes in my direction," *the Look* may also rest with any object which acts as a support for *the Look:* the rustling of branches; the sound of footsteps, followed by silence; the slight opening of a shutter; or, the light movement of a curtain may all be evidence of *the Look.* And as a case in point, Sartre in *Being and*

Nothingness gives the example of brush soldiers who, during an attack, perceive as a look to be avoided "not two eyes, but a white farm-house which is outlined against the sky at the top of a little hill." That the soldiers may be mistaken in that "the objects of the world which I took for eyes were not eyes," in no way reduces their certainty of the existence of the Other. This is shown once more through Sartre's famous spy who, while eavesdropping through a keyhole, discovers that the sound of footsteps has been only a false alarm:

> The Other's existence is so far from being placed in doubt that this false alarm can very well result in making me give up my enterprise. If, on the other hand, I persevere in it, I shall feel my heart beat fast, and I shall detect the slightest creaking of the stairs. Far from disappearing with my first alarm, the Other is present everywhere, below me, above me, in the neighboring rooms, and I continue to feel profoundly my being-for-others. It is even possible that my shame may not disappear; it is my red face as I bend over the keyhole. I do not cease to *experience* my being-for-others; my possibilities do not cease to "die," nor do the distances cease to unfold toward me in terms of the stairway where somebody "could" be in terms of this dark corner where a human presence "could" hide. Better yet, if I tremble at the slightest noise, if each creak announces to me a look, this is because I am already in the state of being-looked-at.[9]

As Sartre goes on to explain, the existence of the Other can never be in doubt because he serves as the foundation of our knowledge of ourselves and because the attitude of shame, as exemplified in the spy, would be non-existent unless there remained the possibility of being seen by the Other and, subsequently, of being transformed into an 'in-itself'. As Sartre defines the ramifications of *the Look:*

> I grasp the Other's look at the very center of my *act* as the solidification and alienation of my own possibilities. In fear or in anxious or prudent anticipation, I perceive that these possibilities which I *am* and which are the condition of my transcendence are given also to another, given as about to be transcended in turn by his own possibilities. The Other as a look is only that—my transcendence transcended.[10]

Given that the aim of the Other is to circumscribe the freedom of another by turning him into an object while, on the other hand, the aim of the subject is to exercise his freedom by turning the Other into an object, man's relationship with the Other is founded on conflict and a bid for power. Simone de Beauvoir in *The Second Sex* re-iterates the themes of Sartre's *Being and Nothingness*. She describes the Other as necessary to one's being; however, that very necessity is contingent upon struggle, given the dichotomous nature of the union:

Once the subject seeks to assert himself, the Other, who limits and denies him, is nonetheless a necessity to him: he attains himself only through that reality which he is not, which is something other than himself. That is why man's life is never abundance and quietude; it is dearth and activity, it is struggle.[11]

On the conception of *The Second Sex*, Deirdre Bair has proffered that

Although she [Beauvoir] cared little what critics said about her, she did want to defend herself without entering the arena of gossip and insult. She thought to do this by writing an essay in which she could define herself personally (as woman) and philosophically (as Existentialist). She intended to relate both to the system Sartre had constructed in *Being and Nothingness*, which she accepted unquestioningly as her own *raison d'être*. Her primary intention was to construct a work that would confuse and embarrass her detractors by its intelligence and dignity, and would gain converts for Sartre by the lucidity and persuasion of her argument.[12]

The novel *She Came to Stay*, by Simone de Beauvoir, dramatizes the perennial struggle with the Other for transcendence. On the philosophical, as well as the autobiographical, nature of *She Came to Stay*, Axel Madsen has written in *Hearts and Minds: The Common Journey of Simone de Beauvoir and Jean-Paul Sartre:*

Pierre was Sartre and Françoise herself. Pierre is an innovative stage director and Françoise his alter ego and theatrical jack-of-all-trades, den mother for insecure actors, late-night typist of new lines of dialogue, critic and essential support to Pierre's talent. She allows him a central and sovereign position in her life and pays the price—losing her definition of herself. The young girl is Xavière, full of irresponsibility, ecstasy and pouting guile. One day when all three are together, Françoise feels herself "exiled" from them, and tries to draw on her own resources for self-support. In vain, for she is without features and individuality. Someone else is stealing the world from her, invading her personality and disfiguring her inner self. To shatter the spell, Françoise kills Xavière.[13]

Such conflict as described by Sartre and affirmed by de Beauvoir as characteristic of human relationships is corroborated in the novel *Fragments* by Ayi Kwei Armah. The young artist-hero, Baako Onipa, wants to become a writer, but society is determined to petrify him into the perfunctory social role of a been-to. Armah has written disparagingly of the been-to in "A Mystification: African Independence Revalued" that "it's a fact that nobody expects this class [the African elite] to do anything than to *be* been-to's, etc., and to consume an intricate heap of privileges."[14] Subsequently, the been-to's feeling of shame, like that of the spy, comes from the recognition that he has an outside or an object-side which is alien to him but which is, nevertheless, part of his original being.

Indications of what the character is expected to become can be gleaned from the chapter "Akwaaba" which describes the respective returns of Henry Robert Hudson Brempong and the artist-hero of the novel. Compared to Baako who has spent five years of study in America, Brempong has spent close to eight years in Great Britain. However, unlike Baako who has to fight back feelings of nausea brought on by his dreaded return home, Brempong exudes the confidence of someone who is in his element. He is both expansive and garrulous, and immediately aboard the plane, Brempong assumes a proprietary air, making during the flight several unnecessary trips to the rear in order to announce his presence to his cabin mates.[15]

When seen alongside the exuberance of Brempong, the morose attitude of Baako serves as quite a contrast. Robert Fraser, in his discussion of the novel, describes Baako's attitude as "not unlike shell-shock," since his decision to return to Ghana has been precipitated by a set of uncontrollable circumstances. He writes:

> You will remember that at this juncture, suspended halfway between New York and Ghana, Baako is in a condition not unlike shell-shock. A disturbance of an unknown but threatening nature has driven him in terror from America, and there has been a recent recurrence in Paris which has sent him scuttling to the airport. Literally and metaphorically, he is in a process of flight. . . . The heavy, mesmerized, almost bleary-eyed feel of both the dog passage and the airport sequence speak of a personal disorientation only heightened by the intellectual lucidity of those it afflicts.[16]

Baako's anxieties are related to perceived shortcomings of himself as a been-to. In conversation with the psychiatrist Juana subsequent to his return, he speaks of the been-to as a modern descendant of traditional myth. In traditional mythology, the man who traveled abroad was regarded as a social hero whose return would be marked by beneficent change for the entire community. However, in the modern-day version of the myth, the community itself is forgotten as the hero is expected to make his immediate family rich, largely at the expense of the community (151).

For Baako, therefore, who returns without the quintessential cargo, thus countering the stereotypical image of a successful been-to, his alienation is assured. For example, a customs official at the airport during Baako's return cannot help remarking the conspicuous lack of cargo (87). Also, idle taxi-cab drivers feign engagement when approached by a character so nondescript in appearance as to be regarded a failure. Brempong, in conversation with Baako earlier, had observed what he considered to be his deficiency as a been-to, namely, his ordinariness (76).

Brempong, on the other hand, is the example *par excellence* of the successful been-to. He personifies what one reviewer has termed in the novel as "trinket worship . . . Ghanaians corruptly devoted to cars, tape recorders and neon 'WELLCOME' signs at airports."[17] Indeed, Brempong's inculcation of European values has been so successful that he has been reduced to a caricature. Aboard the plane Brempong introduces himself to Baako as "Henry Robert Hudson Brempong" (70). He sports a "dark wool suit" and is accompanied by his wife who is identified only by her "generous mass of a wig." In conversation with Baako, he identifies success abroad in terms of material acquisitions and states that an express purpose for traveling abroad is to collect merchandise such as German cars, tape recorders and deep refrigeration plants (83-84).

However, this conversation with Baako notwithstanding, perhaps the most revealing example of Brempong's "trinket worship" is found during Brempong's arrival at the airport. He is given a hero's welcome, is hailed by family and friends as "our white man," "the big man," and, in a gesture rich in symbolism, is anointed their new Messiah (90). Nonetheless, in the midst of this riotous reception, Brempong pauses briefly to exchange parting greetings with Baako, demonstrating, even at this inopportune moment, yet again an absurd obsession with *objects d'art* (91).

In that the character Brempong is made a caricature of European decadence, he is reminiscent of the corrupt politician Joe Koomson in *The Beautyful Ones* who, similarly, has been identified only in terms of his material possessions. As Gareth Griffiths, in the article "Structure and Image in Kwei Armah's *The Beautyful Ones Are Not Yet Born,*" has successfully analyzed:

> Armah dwells on Koomson's suit, which replaces the man entirely. He is the white man because he is a white shirt, gleaming through a darkness into which his body merges. He is literally the gleaming clothes he stands in. . . . The black-white man is invisible because he is merely a caricature. He has no social or economic reality, no personal identity. His reality is defined solely by the objects with which he surrounds himself, and from which he builds "a personality."[18]

To the extent that these characters, Brempong and Koomson, are guilty of evading their personal freedom through an attitude of seriousness, seriousness being a pejorative term used by Sartre to refer to man's dedication to a lot of social principles and prescriptions in denial of his free choice and responsibility, they are identifiable with those Sartre has termed *les lâches* (cowards): "Those who hide from this total freedom, in a guise of solemnity or with deterministic excuses, I shall call cowards."[19]

According to Sartre, man is differentiated from the other objects in the world because he lacks an essence. Unlike the artisan who fashions a paper knife with a definite purpose in mind, man surges up into the world without any prior conception of himself. Since God does not exist, there is no creator to function as "a supernal artisan" and bestow upon him his essence of being. Man simply is. And it is therefore incumbent upon him to ascribe to himself an essence and to legislate his own values:

> For if indeed existence precedes essence, one will never be able to explain one's action by reference to a given and specific nature; in other words, there is no determinism—man is free, man *is* freedom. Nor, on the other hand, if God does not exist, are we provided with any values or commands that could legitimise our behavior. Thus we have neither behind us, nor before us in a luminous realm of values, any means of justification or excuse. We are left alone, without excuse. That is what I mean when I say that man is condemned to be free. Condemned, because he did not create himself, yet he is nevertheless at liberty, and from the moment that he is thrown into this world he is responsible for everything he does.[20]

The responsibility that Sartre speaks of is two-fold. To be sure, man is responsible for creating his own identity; yet, to the degree that all his acts are creative, bespeaking in themselves the kind of person he wills himself to be, they also come to form a conception of man as he believes he ought to be. Sartre explains:

> I decide to marry and to have children; even though this decision proceeds simply from my situation, from my passion or my desire, I am thereby committing not only myself, but humanity as a whole, to the practice of monogamy. I am thus responsible for myself and for all men, and I am creating a certain image of man as I would have him to be. In fashioning myself I fashion man.[21]

The existential anguish which Sartre speaks of comes precisely from man's knowledge that he legislates values not only for himself but for the rest of mankind. And Sartre contends that those who are not in anguish over their personal freedom are either disguising it, or are in flight from it, consequently labeling all those who hide behind social prescriptions and formulaic behavior *les lâches* (cowards). An example of *les lâches* in Sartre's own work is Lucien Fleur of "The Childhood of a Leader," since he prefers the convenient banner of anti-Semitism to the nothingness of the 'for-itself' and, like the Legion of Honour to whom he can be compared, seeks to disguise his personal freedom through the prominent facade of a moustache. As Roquentin had observed in *Nausea:*

The handsome gentleman exists, the Legion of Honour, the moustache exists, it is all; how happy one must be to be nothing more than a Legion of Honour and a moustache and no one sees the rest, he sees the two pointed ends of his moustache on both sides of his nose; I do not think, therefore I am a moustache.[22]

Likewise, in Armah's works *The Beautyful Ones* and *Fragments*, the characters Joe Koomson and Henry Robert Hudson Brempong become representative of *les lâches*, since, like Lucien and the Legion of Honour, they trade their personal liberties for social stereotypes, becoming, by virtue of their materialistic interests, symbols of European decadence, inseparable from such externals as Mercedes saloons, deep refrigeration plants, Moroccan leather purses, and dark wool suits.

The latter, the dark wool suit, is used by Armah in the same manner as the moustache is used by Sartre: to identify those characters who, in their pursuit of social absolutes, jeopardize their personal identities. For example, Brempong of *Fragments* is no more than an African who wants to be European. He not only has assumed an Anglican name, but, worse, having spent practically eight years in England, he now feels entitled to refer to England as "the old country." Therefore, in light of his practice of dissimulation, it is not surprising that he is described in colors, black and white, which essentially highlight his hybrid personality (68). This stock figure of a character is highly reminiscent of another been-to described by Chinua Achebe in *No Longer at Ease* who, upon returning to Nigeria, dons, as his homecoming outfit, "a black suit, bowler hat, and rolled umbrella, even though it was a hot October day."[23]

However, besides dark wool suits, another feature identifiable with Africa's new national middle class as described by Armah is a penchant for over-indulgence which often translates into obesity. Martin Tucker, in his review of *The Beautyful Ones*, recollects the scene at the end of the novel, observing, incidentally, the physical incongruity between the man and Koomson as the latter, now a fallen politician, tries to make his escape. He notes:

There is a way out through the hole in The Man's outhouse. The politician is almost too fat to pass through the eye hole of the dung-heap, while The Man, lean and humble, has no trouble. Finally the fat politician, filled with the stench of corruption, gets through the dung-heap. It is a symbolic dive, matching his manured life.[24]

What appears to be only an implicit parallel of leanness to morality in *The Beautyful Ones*, however, becomes more explicit in *Fragments*. For example, Fifi, a relative of Baako's who now works at Ghana Bank, cannot help noticing the frail appearance of the newly-arrived been-to (103). Furthermore, he cannot quite fathom a been-to without a car

(104-5). Fifi's latter assumption that a been-to would not return without this essential piece of cargo finds an echo in Baako's mother Efua who, promptly after greeting her long-awaited son, asks when his car will arrive, "so that [her] old bones can also rest" (108).

Such an arrant display of materialistic interests, similar to those found in the family of the man in *The Beautyful Ones,* is but added proof of the spiritual penury currently affecting Ghanaian society, the extent of which can be gathered from the various episodes of sterility found contained in the novel.

At Ghanavision, where Baako has taken a job as scriptwriter, hoping "to revolutionize Ghana through creative journalism,"[25] his creative efforts are met repeatedly with barely-disguised disinterest. Asante-Smith, the Director of Ghanavision, remarks Baako's concerns as "too abstract" and "peculiar" and continuously pleads a lack of film for dramatic productions. Film is used to produce documentaries which glorify the nation's leaders. As one associate candidly puts it to Baako: "A nation is built through glorifying its big shots. That's our job anyway" (193).

Another reason for the non-productivity at Ghanavision is the absence of television sets. It is learned that a consignment of sets has been ordered by the officials at Ghanavision, principally to help alleviate the country's need for electronic hardware; nonetheless, when the long-awaited shipment finally arrives, the plan to distribute the sets among the villages is forgotten as the Senior officials form a motorcade to confiscate the public property for their own private use. When the procession ends, a single unattractive set remains, and Baako, the sole abstainer from this corporate theft, witnesses as two junior workmen tussle over the last set before finally destroying it in their jealous bid for possession (219-20).

Grown increasingly weary with the self-aggrandizement of his colleagues at Ghanavision, Baako therefore hastily drafts his letter of resignation and retreats into solitude; nonetheless, this impetuous decision to resign brings little relief from the national malaise as Baako sees that the sterility prevalent at Ghanavision is so widespread as to have affected even the outer regions of the country.

During a drive in the country one afternoon, Juana and Baako stop at a ferry crossing where dozens of trucks and lorries await the ferryboat's final run of the day. One driver with a lorry loaded with plantain and cassava has waited at the landing for three full days and has been unable to make the crossing. Impatient with more fleet-footed drivers and a system that does not work, the driver therefore rams his lorry into the rear of another truck in a desperate attempt to make more room and to force his lorry onto the ferryboat. The gambit fails, however, as with only the front end of the lorry on the ferryboat, the boat pulls away from the landing. The lorry hangs suspended for a moment before crashing into the river, subsequently killing the driver. However, when Baako reports the accident to the engineer-in-charge, the engineer is unmoved. His prime concern is with clearing up the wreckage left by the accident and not with developing strategies that would prevent future occurrences (202).

In light of this benevolent regard for red tape and an unquestioning faith in a set of handed-down procedures which no longer work, Baako is left feeling that human life counts for little, so impoverished has the country become of intellectual resources.

In a later short story "Halfway to Nirvana,"[26] published in 1984, the Anti-Drought Organization, of which Christian Mohamed Tumbo is representative, becomes symbolic of a "mental castration" that has become the legacy of colonialism. The seed for the short story is contained in the article "Flood and famine, drought and glut." The author notes that an inspection of African history will reveal that the natural catastrophes famine, flood, drought, and glut are not unprecedented. The prevention of these natural disasters, however, is what concerns Armah. The author finds in the history of ancient Egypt a cautionary tale; also, a solution to Africa's blight:

> Mane [an ancient Egyptian leader], by unifying all of the 42 *nomes* of North and South Egypt, ended this condition of chronic disunity and distress. For unification made possible the regulated use of natural resources, the national study and adoption of appropriate developmental measures, including the building of dykes, retaining walls, canals and basins, the indispensable groundwork for planned agricultural development. After that there was the construction of storage bins, the stockpiling of reserves for years ahead. . . .
>
> Great as the ancient bounty of the Nile was, it's as nothing compared to the combined wealth represented by Africa's rivers, sun power, soil and subsoil resources. What is missing in Africa today is what was missing in Egypt before the unifying regime of Mane: intelligent, unified social organization.[27]

Ironically, the dearth of intellectual resources on the part of the African elite, as condemned by Armah elsewhere, is exhibited by the members of Baako's own family, particularly on the occasion of the outdooring ceremony. Kirsten Holst Petersen has explained, in the article "Loss and Frustration: An Analysis of A.K. Armah's *Fragments,*" the meaning of the ritual: "Just as Naana must die in order to be reborn a spirit, so babies must die in the spirit world in order to be born as human beings. This explains the meaning of the outdooring ceremony."[28] The birth of Araba's baby, however, provides the family with the perfect excuse for the exploitation of material interests. Soon after the baby is born, he is made the victim of greed. Baako's mother

wants to move ahead the traditional ceremony to have it coincide with
the weekend following payday. Only then can she be certain that the
guests will give generously (131).

The danger of such haste, however, is articulated by Naana, Baako's
grandmother, whose prophecy of doom for the "traveler between the
world of spirits and this one of heavy flesh" emanates from her witness
of the destruction of ancient ritual. As usual, Naana's predictions are
ignored; but, also, as usual, her predictions are correct. The infant,
wrapped in the rich folds of *kente* cloth, with an electric fan to mitigate
the heat, dies suddenly from over-exposure, and, ironically, amidst the
fanfare intended to celebrate its entrance into the world.

Robert Fraser views the infanticide not only as symbolic of the
family's worship of a modernistic deity, to whom the child is ultimately
sacrificed, but also as symbolic of the family's pervasive sterility which
thwarts its power to create. Recalling the scene in chapter two where
an impotent murders a rabid dog, Fraser notes that it forms "a shock
wave" which extends to the outdooring ceremony and, finally, to the
chase scene near the end of the novel where the members of Baako's
family, disappointed in his failure to enrich them, force him into the
asylum. He has written:

> Frustrated masculinity expressing itself as violence: it is a familiar and entirely
> comprehensible formula. In the novel it has reverberations way beyond this
> particular context. One is reminded of the outdooring ceremony, in which a life is
> sacrificed to exorcize a communal impotence. More crucially still, one recalls the
> incident towards the end of the book when, just before his incarceration, Baako
> escapes from the clutches of his family, only to be surrounded by a hectoring,
> bullying crowd who attempt to trap him with ropes. Here again, the implication is
> that Baako has been turned into a scapegoat for the weakness of a whole people
> whose resentment is founded on fear. Indeed if one extends this idea by considering
> the treatment meted out to Baako throughout the novel, one can see the earlier
> episode of the dog as a cogent metaphor for the whole work, held in perfect
> miniature.[29]

It is interesting to note, however, that where, in Fraser's analysis,
Baako has become a victim of impotent society, in a stricter existential
framework, Baako has become a victim of *les salauds*, since his
insanity, by and large, is caused by his rejection of the current moneyed
values sanctioned by *les salauds*. Martin Tucker, in his review, has
analyzed the destructive role played by the mother in the novel. He has
written:

> One of the most significant agents in Baako's destruction is the mother. Her
> dreams of Baako's providing a car and a showy home for her are turned into the
> drab realism of his moving into her small house and taking the bus every morning
> to work like any African commuter. Finally and tragically she fails to understand

Baako's dream of writing; when she discovers his journal and concludes that he is
writing to himself, she rationalizes that he is mad, for only a sick man writes and
speaks to himself. She has her family forcibly take Baako to a mental asylum.[30]

According to Sartre, *les salauds* (swine) are the equals to *les lâches*
(cowards), since they, like *les lâches*, adapt themselves to ready-made
prescriptions, thereby shirking the responsibility of creating their own
lives. However, to the degree that *les salauds* are not satisfied with
their own petrification but, instead, attempt to immobilize the will and
the determination of others to pursue their own projects, they are
considerably worse than *les lâches*. Brian Masters differentiates
between the two:

> Basking in a false tranquillity, blithely sure of themselves, refusing to question
> or doubt that their existence is justified, the *salauds* strive to impose their own
> ancient system of handed-down values on their fellow-men. They claim Right and
> Reason for their own, thus making everyone who does not conform to their order
> feel guilt and inadequacy.[31]

In Sartre's play *The Respectful Prostitute*, both the Negro and the
prostitute are victims of *les salauds*, since both perform, unwittingly, in
accordance with the given stereotype at the expense of their own
integrity. The Negro, wrongfully accused of attempted rape, accepts the
fact that he is a condemned man, despite the fact that he is innocent.
Likewise, the young prostitute who is in a position to help him since
she can testify to his innocence, accepts the fact that she is helpless to
intervene because she cannot escape her classification as a social misfit.
In the end, both conform to a set of standards not of their own making;
both accept as immutable the set of conditions which have made them
outcasts and which have branded them dirt.

Similarly, in both *The Beautyful Ones* and *Fragments*, the man,
Teacher, and Baako Onipa are victims of *les salauds*, since their
respective guilt, despair, and insanity are directly linked to the collective
attempt of family and society to force them to honor a corrupt system
of values. On the latter, Cecil Abrahams, in the article "Perspectives on
Africa," explains the dilemma of Baako Onipa in terms of the
character's money-making potential, paralleling it to that of the real-life
artist: "Like Baako, Armah had returned to Ghana without the material
things his family expected him to have. Like Baako, as Armah told me,
he was regarded as insane by his relatives for wanting to be an artist
and not a materialistic politician."[32]

An example of the cupidity referred to here by Abrahams is found in
the chapter "Efua." During Baako's confinement to the asylum, he
recalls, with shame, the disappointment of his mother Efua who had
begun building a monumental structure in celebration of her son's

homecoming. The edifice, however, had gone uncompleted because Baako "had seen no need to go off into huge mansions and inflate himself to fill the space" (251). Instead, he had been content to move into the modest family bungalow which had already housed his blind grandmother Naana, his sister Araba, his brother-in-law Kwesi, and his mother Efua. The mother, gradually realizing that the huge structure would never be completed, had finally exorcised all hope and had given up on what had, by now, manifested itself as a lost cause (254).

The extent of the destructive influence caused by *les salauds* is shown at the end of the novel. There, Baako, a psychotic, confined to the Acute Ward of an insane asylum, has his alienation now complete. He refers to himself disparagingly as "the foolish one" (252), "the clown" (260), and looks upon his moral fastidiousness as but another form of hubris (252).

On the other hand, the extent of the destructive influence caused by *les salauds* may be seen in *The Beautyful Ones* in the self-deprecating tones of the likewise morally upright man who, when confronted with "this flat look" in Oyo's eyes that is "a defense against hope" (41), experiences himself as a consummate failure. He confesses to Teacher:

> "What I don't understand," he said, "is my own feeling about it. I know I have done nothing wrong. I could even get angry with Oyo about this. And yet, I am the one who feels strange."
> "The condemned man."
> "Yes. I feel like a criminal. Often these days I find myself thinking of something sudden I could do to redeem myself in their eyes. Then I sit down and ask myself what I have done wrong, and there is really nothing." (53)

Likewise, the defeat of Teacher is represented in the designation of himself as a cipher, or ghost, worthy only of familial disinheritance. Teacher admits to nightmares of himself as the prodigal son returning home, only to be scorned by his now rich and successful mother for his past history of negligence. He shares with the man his shame and despair:

> "With a companion who shared all my soul's desires I had come from a long way off, seeking refuge with my mother in her house. The mansion was very large. There was room, lots of room, in it, but when I spoke to my mother she seemed torn within by an impossible decision. But then she made up her mind, and out of her ran a stream of words, every drop filled with all the resentment and the hate of her long disappointment with me. 'Yes, you have come to rest here, you who have put nothing here at all. So how much money have you given me in all your life, and how much help? And now you come here, here, here.' When her anger grew unbearable she drove me out into the street outside." (59)

The destructive impact of *les salauds* leads Sartre to consider all relationships based upon conflict. Anthony Manser in his book, *Sartre: A Philosophic Study,* sees as an example of this on-going competition with the Other "the battle of looks of two people passing in an empty street; each tries 'to stare the other down.' The victor in this encounter can look at the other without himself being looked at."[33] Similarly, Alfred Stern in *Sartre: His Philosophy and Existential Psychoanalysis* contends that "to dress oneself means to dissimulate our object-character, to claim the right to see without being seen, the right to be a mere subject."[34]

In Sartre's play *No Exit,* an example of this fierce rivalry with the Other is demonstrated. The characters, Joseph Garcin, Inez Serrano, and Estelle Rigault, condemned to Hell because of their exploitation of others, now must endure, as their own punishment, their objectification by the Other. Garcin, a pacifist and war deserter who had victimized his wife because "it was so easy," finds now that he must suffer as his punishment the unmitigated scorn of Inez who views him as a coward. Similarly, Estelle Rigault, a *femme fatale* responsible for both the death of her illegitimate baby and, inadvertently, for the death of her lover, must tolerate now as her form of punishment the petrification of herself as an infanticide in the eyes of Garcin. And, finally, Inez, a lesbian whose sadistic tendencies had driven her lover one night to turn on the gas and murder them both, finds now that she must suffer as her own particular brand of punishment the petrification of herself in the eyes of Estelle as a non-entity. As Estelle explains to Garcin the reason for her rejection of the amorous overtures made by Inez: "'But she doesn't count, she's a woman.'"[35] In essence, each character is bound to the Other by the nature of his persecution, and each is forced to pursue, without cessation or without any hope of success, the vindication of himself or herself from the polluted image formed by the Other. As Dorothy McCall explains "this unlivable solidarity" of the characters in Hell:

> As the play circles downward and inward to its conclusion, the three realize in horror their complete interdependence. "I don't suppose if God had given us the clear knowledge of how closely we are bound to one another," Bernanos writes in *The Diary of a Country Priest,* "that we could go on living." As the layers of lies are torn away, the three "others" of *No Exit* are given a clear knowledge of this unlivable solidarity. Each is at the mercy of another who will not give him what he wants and can get only from that one person. Inez wants Estelle who wants Garcin who wants the reassurance of Inez. Every move of one of the three, in word or gesture, sets the cycle of punishment repeating its inevitable round. Inez and Estelle will eternally desire and be frustrated; Garcin will eternally seek his impossible salvation.[36]

The pronouncement made by Garcin at the end of the play, a
pronouncement that is crucial to Sartre's statement of theme, comes
precisely from Garcin's recognition that his self-esteem is contingent
upon the approval of Inez. As he concedes the true meaning of Hell:
"'So this is hell. I'd never have believed it. You remember all we were
told about the torture-chambers, the fire and brimstone, the 'burning
marl.' Old wives' tales! There's no need for red-hot pokers. Hell is--
other people!'"[37]

In an interview with Axel Madsen, Sartre was to clarify the meaning
of the line from *No Exit:*

> "People think I mean that our relationships with others are always poisoned. What
> I mean is that our relationships are always twisted, always spoiled and perverted.
> But other people are also what is most important in ourselves; without someone else
> none of us can understand himself. The three characters are of course dead since
> they are in hell and I wanted the public watching the 'living dead' on the stage to
> realize that to surround yourself with judgments and actions you can do nothing
> about, is also to be a living dead. I wanted to show, ad absurdum, the importance
> of free will, that one action can be changed by another. Whatever the infernal circle
> we live in, I think we are free to break out of it. And those who don't break out
> remain where they are *also* by free choice. They create their own hell voluntarily.
> The play is about relationships that get rusty and fossilize and about freedom—
> freedom as a barely suggested flipside."[38]

On the other hand, in the literature by Ayi Kwei Armah, one finds
no such strong pronouncement of theme. Armah's concerns rest largely
with the pernicious effects of Africa's contact with the Western world
and, concurrently, with the alienation felt by the characters caught up
in this confusion of contemporary values. Nonetheless, inasmuch as
Armah's themes are invariably social, treating as they do the plight of
characters amid a modern-day spiritual crisis, man's fractured, or
perverted, relationship with the Other ultimately emerges as a natural
attendant of his major concern.

1. Jean-Paul Sartre, "The Room," in *Intimacy and Other Stories*, trans. Lloyd Alexander (New York: New Directions, 1948), 60-61.

2. Jean-Paul Sartre, *Being and Nothingness: An Essay in Phenomenological Ontology*, intro. and trans. Hazel Barnes (New York: Philosophical Library, 1956), 259.

3. Ibid., 259.

4. Ibid., 261.

5. Ibid., lxv.

6. Jean-Paul Sartre, *Nausea*, trans. Lloyd Alexander (New York: New Directions, 1964), 128.

7. Rene Lafarge, *Jean-Paul Sartre: His Philosophy*, trans. Marina Smyth-Kok (Notre Dame: University of Notre Dame Press, 1967), 118-19.

8. Sartre, *Being and Nothingness*, 263.

9. Ibid., 277.

10. Ibid., 263.

11. Simone de Beauvoir, *The Second Sex*, trans. H. M. Parshley (New York: Alfred A. Knopf, 1952), 129.

12. Deirdre Bair, *Simone de Beauvoir: A Biography* (New York: Summit, 1990), 381.

13. Axel Madsen, *Hearts and Minds: The Common Journey of Simone de Beauvoir and Jean-Paul Sartre* (New York: William Morrow and Company, 1977), 84.

14. Ayi Kwei Armah, "A Mystification: African Independence Revalued," *Pan-African Journal 2*, no. 2 (spring 1969): 146.

15. Ayi Kwei Armah, *Fragments* (New York: Collier Books, 1969), 69. All subsequent references to this edition will appear in the text.

16. Robert Fraser, *The Novels of Ayi Kwei Armah* (London: Heinemann, 1980), 43-44.

17. "Is Blindness Best?," *Time*, 2 February 1970, 72.

18. Gareth Griffiths, "Structure and Image in Kwei Armah's *The Beautyful Ones Are Not Yet Born*," *Studies in Black Literature 2*, no. 2 (1971): 3.

19. Jean-Paul Sartre, *Existentialism and Humanism*, intro. and trans. Philip Mairet (London: Methuen, 1948), 52.

20. Ibid., 34.

21. Ibid., 30.

22. Sartre, *Nausea*, 101.

23. Chinua Achebe, *No Longer at Ease* (London: Heinemann, 1960), 27.

24. Martin Tucker, "Tragedy of a Been-to," *The New Republic* 162, no. 31 (January 1970): 24.

25. Charles E. Nnolim, "Dialectic as Form: Pejorism in the Novels of Armah," in *African Literature Today: Retrospect and Prospect* 10 (1979): 220.

26. Ayi Kwei Armah, "Halfway to Nirvana," *West Africa*, 24 September 1984, 1947-48.

27. Ayi Kwei Armah, "Flood and famine, drought and glut," *West Africa*, 30 September 1985, 2012.

28. Kirsten Holst Petersen, "Loss and Frustration: An Analysis of A.K. Armah's *Fragments,*" *Kunapipi* 1, no. 1 (1979): 55.

29. Fraser, *The Novels of Ayi Kwei Armah, 42.*

30. Tucker, 26.

31. Brian Masters, *Sartre: A Study* (London: Heinemann, 1974), 31.

32. Cecil Abrahams, "Perspectives on Africa," in *Canadian Journal of African Studies* 11 (1977): 357.

33. Anthony Manser, *Sartre: A Philosophic Study* (London: Athlone Press, 1966), 77.

34. Alfred Stern, *Sartre: His Philosophy and Existential Psychoanalysis,* 2nd ed., rev. and enl. (New York: Delacorte Press, 1967), 152.

35. Jean-Paul Sartre, *No Exit,* in *No Exit and Three Other Plays* (New York: Knopf, 1948), 34.

36. Dorothy McCall, "No Exit," in *The Theatre of Jean-Paul Sartre* (New York: Columbia University Press, 1967), 114-15.

37. Sartre, *No Exit,* 46-47.

38. Axel Madsen, 112-13.

Chapter 4

The Narcissism of the Intellectual Hero

In order to escape the uncertainty of the 'for-itself' and the alienation which may result from making one's own self or "doing one's own thing," as witnessed in the man and Teacher in *The Beautyful Ones Are Not Yet Born* and Baako in *Fragments,* one may decide, like Koomson in *The Beautyful Ones* and Brempong in *Fragments,* to take refuge in a prescribed system of values rather than confront "a virgin future." In *Existentialism and Humanism* Sartre uses the term "abandonment" to describe the absolute freedom of the 'for-itself'. Alone in the world without deference to any higher authority, man has to take full responsibility for his actions. He has no recourse to fatalism or determinism, since he wills himself, simultaneously creating in the process his personal system of values. Sartre explains in *Existentialism and Humanism:*

> For if indeed existence precedes essence, one will never be able to explain one's action by reference to a given and specific human nature; in other words, there is no determinism—man is free, man *is* freedom. Nor, on the other hand, if God does not exist, are we provided with any values or commands behind us, nor before us in a luminous realm of values, any means of justification or excuse. We are left alone, without excuse. That is what I mean when I say that man is condemned to be free. Condemned, because he did not create himself, yet he is nevertheless at liberty, and from the moment that he is thrown into this world he is responsible for everything he does.[1]

An example of this state of abandonment is found in a former student of Sartre's. In *Existentialism and Humanism* Sartre describes a young man who was torn between avenging the memory of his brother who had been killed in "the German offensive of 1940" by enlisting in the armed services or staying with his bereaved and dejected mother who had left his collaborationist father. Without recourse to Christian

doctrine or ethical scripture, the young man had come to Sartre seeking
advice, the visit itself, though, signaling a chosen course of action:

> In coming to me, he knew what advice I should give him, and I had but one reply
> to make. You are free, therefore choose--that is to say, invent. No role of general
> morality can show you what you ought to do: no signs are vouchsafed in this
> world.[2]

The anguish and despair so common to the literature by Sartre
proceed directly from this absolute sense of abandonment in the world;
from the recognition that one is entirely self-governed, alienated from
the other by one's individual projects, desires, and interests. Sartre
relates in *Existentialism and Humanism:* "I cannot count upon men
whom I do not know, I cannot base my confidence upon human
goodness or upon man's interest in the good of society, seeing that man
is free and that there is no human nature which I can take as
foundational."[3]

Because existentialism is a philosophy identified with freedom,
choice, and responsibility, Sartre is critical of those individuals who
hide behind social facades and prescriptive social behavior, thus hoping
to eliminate the anguish which comes from creating themselves.
Although he concedes that an existentialist mode of thought defies
moral judgement, recognizing that each individual is responsible for his
own set of values, Sartre nonetheless makes "a logical judgment" based
upon the pre-conditions of his atheistic philosophy, concluding that
unreasonable faith in a doctrinaire system of values is both cowardly
and self-deceptive: "Since we have defined the situation of man as one
of free choice, without excuse and without help, any man who takes
refuge behind the excuse of his passions, or by inventing some
deterministic doctrine, is a self-deceiver."[4]

The cowardice which Sartre identifies with attitudes of determinism
may be seen in Lucien Fleur of "Childhood of a Leader," Joe Koomson
of *The Beautyful Ones,* and Henry Robert Hudson Brempong of
Fragments. It may be seen also in Mathieu Delarue of Sartre's *The Age
of Reason* and Solo Nkonam of Armah's *Why Are We So Blest?.*
However, unlike their predecessors whose cowardice had social impetus,
the cowardice of the latter is more the product of their own obsessive
self-contemplation.

Victor Brombart, in his work *The Intellectual Hero,* has referred to
"lucidity" as "the particular curse of the Sartrean intellectual."[5] That
is, not only is the Sartrean intellectual "forever in search of a witness-
judge,"[6] but he also rather sadistically seeks to become his own
persecutor or witness-judge through his uncompromising introspection
and judgement. In *Being and Nothingness* Sartre had described

reflection as the individual's attempt to become his own foundation or "self-cause" by positing himself as an object for the 'for-itself': "By reflection the for-itself, which has lost itself outside itself, attempts to put itself inside its own being. Reflection is a second effort by the for-itself to found itself; that is, to be for itself what it is."[7] However, because the 'for-itself' can neither escape the contingency of being, nor can it recover itself as a given, or 'a nihilated in-itself', reflection always remains a deception or failure:

> This effort to be to itself its own foundation, to recover and to dominate within itself its own flight, finally to be that flight instead of temporalizing it as the flight which is fled—this effort inevitably results in failure; and it is precisely this failure which is reflection.[8]

While acknowledging that reflection and introspection are characteristics of the Sartrean intellectual, Brombart qualifies his observation by noting that it is "a perverted form of mental narcissism which impels him to search for his most unflattering image."[9] Brombart had linked the self-doubt, contempt and denunciation common to the intellectual hero to the social and political climate in France which had stigmatized the intellectuals as arrogant anarchists. In the introduction to his work Brombart had related the observations of some early French critics:

> [Maurice] Barrès calls all intellectuals *déracinés* (uprooted). Lucien Herr, in the *Revue Blanche,* rejoins that they are *désintéressés* (selfless). *Déracinés* or *désintéressés,* uprooted or selfless—the argument implies nothing less than a difference of perspective. To the ones, the intellectual is the sworn enemy of the collective discipline, the enemy of the established social order. . . . To the others, this supposed corrosive and subversive force is but proof of their moral dynamism, of the integrity of their critical stand and of their competence to serve as liaison agents between one culture and another.[10]

Because of society's often unflattering portrait of the intellectual, Brombart concludes that the intellectual often conceives of himself in ambivalent, often contradictory terms. Particularly in the literature by Jean-Paul Sartre and Simone de Beauvoir, Brombart notes qualities of narcissism and impotence. For example, on the unflattering image of the intellectual portrayed by Sartre in his fiction, Brombart concludes: "The typical Sartrean character is the intellectual; his characteristic mood is one of shame and guilt."[11]

Examples of these unflattering self-portraits may be found in Hugo of *Dirty Hands,* a young Communist rebel who carries around in his suitcase haunting reminders of his bourgeois past, and in Mathieu Delarue of *The Age of Reason,* a pacifist who conceives of himself as "a wash out," "a rotter," an ineffectual intellectual who has led a "toothless" existence.   In *The Mandarins*, a novel by Simone de Beauvoir, the intellectuals Henri Perron and Robert Dubreuilh are examples of "the impotence of the French intellectuals," as they find difficult the justification of esthetes in a post-war world that seems poised on the brink of nuclear, or atomic, destruction:

> The thought of death had never bothered Henri, but suddenly that lunar silence terrified him. Mankind would be no more! In face of that deaf-and-dumb eternity, what earthly sense was there in setting words on paper, holding meetings? You had only to sit back and silently await the universal cataclysm, or your own insignificant death. Nothing meant anything.[12]

Subsequently, they collectively dabble in leftist, or socialist, politics, write political tracts for the newspaper *L'Espoir* that Henri has founded that do not alter the political landscape, and organize a counter-revolutionary movement, the S.R.L., to oppose the Communist Party but whose opposition is tolerated by the Party only as it proves ineffective: "Opposition isn't permitted us except insofar as it has no effectiveness."[13]   For his part, Henri, after a decision to abandon art, is inspired to write a play, *The Survivors*, after witnessing first-hand the devastation of war in the village Vercors.   Its political diffidence, however, foments only divisiveness.   Further, its production fuels speculation that Perron has sold out to the right:

> He [Perron] had made a clean break with Dubreuilh, the S.R.L. had disavowed him, and most of his old comrades felt a shiver of shame when they thought of him. At *L'Enclume*, Lachaume and his friends—and how many others throughout France—were calling him a traitor.[14]

In the literature by Ayi Kwei Armah this same "perverted form of narcissism" may be found in Teacher of *The Beautyful Ones Are Not Yet Born*, who views himself as "one of the dead people, the walking dead"; in Baako Onipa of *Fragments*, who views his morality as excessive pride; and in Solo Nkonam of *Why Are We So Blest?*, who deprecatingly regards himself as an *assimilado*, a black-white man who has fully inculcated Western values.
In one of the early entries to the novel *Why Are We So Blest?*, Solo has admitted that his personal failure has stemmed from his idealism and hypersensitive awareness.   An adopted Congherian educated in Lisbon, Solo had taken refuge in revolution only after a broken affair with a twenty-three-year-old Portuguese female named Sylvia.   His involvement in revolutionary activity, spurred partly as it had been by selfish and romantic reasons, had proved, therefore, a failure.   Solo found that he lacked the "hard entrails" of a militant and that his own

divided sense of self had served to undermine an already dubious attempt at revolutionary commitment.[15]

Implicit in Solo's remembrances is the dilemma which faces him as a would-be African writer. That is, Solo would write a poetic novella, springing from the love of an African student and a Portuguese female; however, fearing in a time when nationalistic sentiment is high that the romantic themes which concern him may be construed as counterrevolutionary, Solo, mistrustful of his own aims, therefore writes nothing and experiences, as a result, a creativity turned inward against himself to become a debilitating and paralyzing disease (13).

Related to Solo's attraction to Western art has been also his aforementioned attraction to the Portuguese female Sylvia, an attraction which he has subsequently interpreted as yet another symptom of the affliction affecting the assimilated African. According to Solo, the assimilated African, alienated from the millions of Africans by privilege, finds that the price of such privilege is often loneliness, "oppression's symptom of success." Looking for companionship and friendship, the African therefore searches the ranks of his oppressors, only to discover a loss of identity and spiritual death (207). Recognizing the implications of his fatal affair with Sylvia, Solo therefore cannot bring himself to play the role of spoilsport in a newly-independent nation caught up in the general euphoria of nationalism (230).

To dissipate the restless energy within himself, Solo therefore attempts to bury himself in translations for the *Jeune Nation,* but finds though in this idle work even greater anxiety and frustration, since his role as a would-be writer is irrevocably reduced to that of consumer (54). O.S. Ogede in the article "Armah in America" argues that Solo's "spiritual uprootedness" is revealed in the character's abstracted use of language:

> [Solo] displays immense facility with language but his goal does not extend beyond exploiting the possibilities of language—its sound patterns—for musical effect only, as in the episode where he takes an aerial view of Laccryville in the company of the young engineer, or in the library scene with the one-legged man who had fought in the country's wars of independence. The absence of proverbial usage in Solo's language, such as is habitual even with a detribalized figure like Obi Okonkwo in Achebe's *No Longer At Ease,* points up the degree of Solo's spiritual uprootedness.[16]

The knowledge of his two-fold failure both as a would-be writer and as a revolutionary hence prevents Solo from warning Modin, another intellectual and would-be revolutionary, against the disillusioned path that he himself has taken. Rationalizing his silence as impotence, since the only alternative which he can offer to the revolutionary commitment which Modin seeks is "the cowed world of *Jeune Nation,*" Solo therefore does nothing but passively marks time, keeping silent vigil over Modin's already-dead remains. Part of Solo's disillusionment had come from his recognition of the spuriousness of many of the revolutionary slogans and pronouncements; from his recognition of the compulsive desire of many of the revolutionaries to get ahead through corrupt means. Indeed, the thematic focus of *Why Are We So Blest?* differs little from that of Armah's previous two novels, namely, that of the betrayal of the African peoples by their nationalist leaders to European interests. In his critical work, *The Novels of Ayi Kwei Armah*, Robert Fraser speaks of the betrayal of the nationalists to propagandistic concerns:

> The Algeria towards which these distracted exiles have gravitated is not a country which would seem to lend any support to their highest ideals. It is independent, but poverty, degradation, mutilation are observable everywhere. The sense one has is that this desolation is due, not simply to the inevitable dislocation of a recent war, but rather to a sell-out by the new national government which is so anxious to court French and international favour that it has neglected the more pressing task of revitalizing the economy.[17]

Evidence of the abandonment of the general populace of Algeria may be found in the opening pages of the novel. An exile from his homeland, Ghana, Solo describes the omnipresence of the beggars, particularly the orphan children, whose hunger has reduced them to vultures. For example, Solo recalls encountering beggars at least one on every block, with the thicker concentrations in heavily trafficked areas, and being waylaid by orphan beggars pleading for a hand-out (16).

Ironically, the difference separating Solo from the beggars to whom he gives alms is the unsettling awareness of his assimilation. Similar to the greedy politicians in *The Beautyful Ones* who have been given the image by Armah of resting upon the backs of the poor, Solo's good fortune and station have likewise been fraudulent, arrived at by the symbolic renouncement of his African heritage and culture and his subsequent acceptance of European values. The result of his renouncement, though, is a profound sense of guilt which tries to ease itself through self-induced maladies which often require hospitalization.

When Solo is hospitalized, though, hoping to escape the guilt related to the poverty surrounding him, he is confronted yet again with the victimization of the innocent caused by the ravages of war. During his recuperation, he visits the hospital library in search of some recreational reading. While there he comes across an amputee who is maniacally examining the shelves as though he were searching for something on which his life depended. When Solo questions him on the nature of his search, he learns that the amputee is searching for books on the French

Revolution, not to find out who was in the revolution but simply to discover who won (24).

Later, as Solo returns to his hospital bed, it is the amputee who approaches him, still seeking some small justification for the revolution he has fought in at no small personal cost. Acknowledging that it is not the militants who gained, since all the best ones died, the cripple is left with the feeling that his war effort has been for naught. Solo, while conceding along with the cripple the inevitable perversion of his revolutionary aims through the petty greed and corruption of upstart politicians, is, nevertheless, able to render some small consolation by representing the militants as the very life-blood or essence of society. In a diagram he depicts society as a massive weight or truck being pushed along from one steep incline to the next by the militants, who represent the fuel, "something pure, light, even spiritual, which consumes itself to push forward something heavier, far more gross than itself" (27).

An example of an opportunist in the novel is Jorge Manuel, "Foreign Minister of the Congherian Government in Exile," whose aping of European ways is symbolically noted in the huge display at the Bureau of the People's Union of Congheria.

As a newcomer to the revolution, Solo had noticed, not without some chagrin, the pictorial history displayed at the office of the UPC. Encaptioned "LE PEUPLE CONGHERIEN EN LUTTE," the display panel had documented the development of the revolutionary army from a rudimentary guerilla outfit to a serious, disciplined and well-organized force. Striking, however, about the display had been the dress of the military leaders which, upon ascendancy, had become lighter, culminating finally in the picture of "IGNACE SENDOULWA: PREMIER MILITANT" who was shown wearing an immaculate white suit. Solo recalled the display saddening him through its implicit equation of discipline, order, and supremacy with "whiteness"; however, rather than admit to the irony of this stubborn entrenchment of European values, even amongst those supposedly committed to the revolution of Africa, Solo had conveniently adopted the attitude of blindness in the face of this unsettling truth (48-49).

In the article "A Mystification: African Independence Revalued," Ayi Kwei Armah debunks the myths surrounding African independence, one of which is that independence automatically led to political sovereignty for African countries. He cites the widening gap between the social classes as evidential of the legerdemain of African independence:

> Independence, far from diminishing the social distance inherent in the superior-inferior metropolitan-provincial relationship, has both increased it and made it more definitely manifest within the African provincial subsystem. The new African

managers of the imperial subsystem in the provinces, the African elite, expanding
under the nationalist leadership umbrella, form a class whose special attribute is its
success in appropriating to itself the social distance maintained between the superior
metropole and the inferior province.[18]

The concerns raised by Armah in his prose and fiction have been
expressed by some West Indian authors as well, namely the Barbadian
author George Lamming in his novel *In the Castle of My Skin*.
Lamming has labeled the ruling elite "the custodial class," since their
role as functionaries in the newly-independent nations is to maintain the
status quo.[19] In his 1983 introduction to *In the Castle of my Skin*, he
has remarked, "the tactical withdrawal which the British now so proudly
call decolonization simply made way for a new colonial
orchestration."[20]

In *In the Castle of My Skin*, the new order is represented by Mr.
Slime, a dismissed school teacher who ventures into local politics. He
opens the Penny Bank, "the depository of the poor man's penny," with
the mission of making the villagers landowners, but ends up robbing
them twice over. Not only does he pilfer their savings in order to
purchase the property from the landowner Creighton, but he offers them
the opportunity to buy back the land at prices which they can ill afford.
Thus he ruins the villagers' hopes of becoming property owners through
the very means which they have afforded him while he furthers his own
ambitions. In that his ascension to village landlord has been the result
of artifice, Mr. Slime is a counterpart of Modin in Ayi Kwei Armah's
Why Are We So Blest? whose Western education has been contingent
upon his ability to masquerade as an atypical African (120).

The reality of this symbolic dichotomy, of superior and inferior, is
represented in *Why Are We So Blest?* by the mulatto Jorge Manuel,
head of the office of UPC. Portuguese-educated, as has been Solo,
Manuel has assumed all of the trappings of the African elite. Not only
has he taken on the all-important title of "Foreign Minister of the
Congherian Government in Exile," but he also has established lush
office quarters on the upper level of the office of UPC for the sole
purpose of receiving international newspapermen and entertaining
African dignitaries. His African assistant, on the other hand, occupies
the austere downstairs office where he routinely performs the daily tasks
of typing correspondence, addressing envelopes, posting letters, and
cutting out newspaper clippings related to the revolution. And that
Manuel is described as "half Portuguese" and Ngulo, his assistant, as
"the dark, silent African" is not to be lost on the reader. Indeed, Solo
finds in this odd coupling of superior and inferior, mulatto and African,
a blatant form of African elitism which threatens the very concept of
nationalism (51-52).

Manuel's life of luxury and ease may be paralleled to that of another opportunist, namely Joe Koomson, labourer-turned politician in *The Beautyful Ones*, whose political posturing is manifest from his association with the Ideological Institute of Winneba, "the instant breeding ground for party hacks."[21] The man relates to his friend Teacher in *The Beautyful Ones*:

> "I still do not know how Koomson got to Accra. Everybody says with a wave of the hand, 'Oh, you know, the ideological thing. Winneba.' True. . . . Men who know nothing about politics have grown hot with ideology, thinking of the money that will come. The civil servant who hates socialism is there, singing hosanna. The poet is there, serving power and waiting to fill his coming paunch with crumbs. . . . Everybody who wants speed goes there and the only thing demanded of them is that they be good at fawning. . . ."[22]

Modin's mistake has been to idealize revolution--to assume that those involved in the cause of African independence would be naturally less susceptible to the forms of prostitution common to the historical factor; but as the wiser Solo later explains to Modin, revolution for the officials at the office of UPC has often been a stepping stone to self-serving political ends (260).

Hence, the susceptibility of African Freedom Fighters to Western influence in the form of personal aggrandizement would account for Modin's inevitable disillusionment; it would also account for Solo's overwhelming sense of impotence, since he recognizes that his weak warnings to Modin are but the pathetic cries of a man likewise condemned (84).

In *Being and Nothingness* Sartre had argued that the past was "irremediable"; that one could no more escape from having a past than one could escape from breathing. To be alive was to have a past, e.g., to have had whooping cough at age five, to have been trained as a military officer at a naval academy, to have entered into a marriage contract, to have purchased a house and started a family. The past was unalterable; however, in that the 'for-itself' made the past exist by consciously surpassing it towards the future, just as the 'for-itself' made the objects of the world exist by bringing them into consciousness, to deliberately give ascendancy to the 'in-itself' was in Sartre's view tantamount to practicing bad faith, since it involved the shirking of responsibility inherent in the 'for-itself' for the determinism of an objectified being, the 'in-itself'. In *Being and Nothingness* Sartre had made the following distinctions between the past as "a free choice of the future" and the past as a chosen solidarity:

> (That which is past is a certain kind of engagement with respect to the past and a certain kind of tradition). On the other hand, there are other for-itselfs whose

project implies the rejection of time and a narrow solidarity with the past. In their desire to find a solid ground these latter have, by contrast, chosen the past as that which they are, everything else being only an indefinite and unworthy flight from tradition. They have chosen *at the start* the refusal of flight; that is, *the refusal to refuse*. The past consequently has the function of requiring of them a fidelity. Thus we shall see that the former persons admit scornfully and easily to a mistake which they have made whereas the very admission will be impossible for the others without their deliberately changing their fundamental project; the latter will then employ all the bad faith in the world and all the subterfuges which they can invent in order to avoid breaking that faith in "what is" which constitutes an essential structure of their project.[23]

The bad faith of Solo with respect to his past is seen in his view of himself as an *assimilado* or a "factor" which he uses, in turn, as an excuse for his failures. More specifically, he excuses his inability to help Modin, citing his own cowardice (83). However, such an attitude, by acceding to the past an absolute value, perpetuates the very claims it theoretically rejects and becomes a rationalization to continue in bad faith. Sartre has noted in *Existential Psychoanalysis:* "A person frees himself from himself by the very act by which he makes himself an object for himself."[24] Given therefore the bad faith of Solo's reflection, he becomes comparable to the closet homosexual in Sartre's *Existential Psychoanalysis* and Daniel Sereno, the pederast, in Sartre's trilogy who likewise use rigid self-analyses in an attempt to both exorcise and exonerate their pattern of social deviance. The duplicity involved in such self-recrimination, however, is revealed in the following:

"Doctor Jekyll and Mr. Hyde. . . ." Daniel envisaged himself with disgust: he felt, within himself, so benevolent, so truly benevolent that it wasn't natural. "That," he thought, "is the real man," with a sort of satisfaction. His was a hard, forbidding character, but underneath it all was a shrinking victim pleading for mercy. It was odd, he thought, that a man could hate himself as though he were someone else. . . . When he despised himself he had the feeling of detachment from his own being, as though he were poised like an impartial judge above a noisome turmoil; then suddenly he found himself plunging downwards, caught again in his own toils.[25]

The ever-present threat of the past, or the 'facticity' of the 'in-itself' to absorb consciousness or the constant flux of the 'for-itself', is represented in the symbol of the viscous, the slimy, or in nausea, which in Sartre's ontology becomes identified with the half-way point between the liquidity of the 'for-itself' and the solidification of the 'in-itself'. Sartre describes in *Existential Psychoanalysis* the connotative value of the viscous: "The slimy reveals itself as essentially ambiguous because its fluidity exists in slow motion; there is a sticky thickness in its liquidity; it represents in itself a dawning triumph of the solid over the liquid."[26]

The correlation of the viscous to Solo's identification of himself as a human "factor" is revealed in the opening pages of the novel. Surrounded by a mass of beggars, adult and children alike, in a country devastated by war, Solo cannot avoid looking upon his life of relative ease with the same disdain and open hostility of those whose daily existence is a gamble, dependent entirely upon the fortuitous good will and generosity of passers-by. He recalls making daily trips to and from the grocer and butcher's, for instance, and feeling like "an overfed pig" because his lifestyle, rather than being determined by need like that of many of the beggars who populate the streets of Algiers, consists of mere indulgences. The result of his profound sense of economic estrangement is guilt and anxiety which manifest themselves in sensations of nausea (21).

The threat of the 'in-itself' to absorb the 'for-itself' is also symbolized in images of floating, which Sartre likewise associates with the viscous. In Sartre's novel *Nausea* Roquentin cannot differentiate himself from the 'in-itself' or from the teeming gobs of matter in the world "all in disorder--naked, in a frightful obscene nakedness," and becomes so repelled by the superfluousness of existence that he conceives of himself, of all matter, as *de trop*, "in the way," and comes to identify his body as a weightless, half-solidified entity capable of floating:

> Mounting up, mounting up as high as the sky, spilling over, filling everything with its gelatinous slither, and I could see depths upon depths of it reaching far beyond the limits of the garden, the houses, and Bouville, as far as the eye could reach. I was no longer in Bouville, I was nowhere, I was floating.[27]

In the context of the novel "floating" becomes associated with both the absurd, with the lack of meaning Roquentin finds in the universe, as well as with Roquentin's taste of himself, with his experience of himself wholly as a body, as an 'in-itself' or object in the world. In effect, it becomes associated with the quality of the viscous or with Roquentin's giddy sensation of being neither/nor--neither completely an 'in-itself' as a chair or table is an 'in-itself', nor an absolute, unencumbered freedom. Alfred Stern has thus characterized the viscous:

> To demonstrate his Existential psychoanalysis of qualities, he [Sartre] could have chosen any quality. If he chose viscosity, it was because it is the symbol of nausea and our whole nauseous existence, in which the ego, the free being-for-itself, is again and again threatened with absorption by the being-in-itself, the absurd, contingent, brute thinghood which stagnates and solidifies the liquidity of our freedom. For the liquidity, or fluidity, of water is the symbol of our consciousness, our freedom; and the slackening of this liquidity, its stagnation and growing solidification into the stickiness of the viscous, is the symbol of our collapse into thinghood, the loss of our freedom and our human condition.[28]

In Ayi Kwei Armah's *Why Are We So Blest?* the images of the viscous, of vomit, nausea and floating, likewise dominate the novel, serving to identify, thematically, the non-being of the character Solo. More specifically, the images of floating serve to identify the character as an 'in-itself' or *assimilado,* a hybrid personality, neither completely black nor white, trapped within its own destructive cycle of love-hate relations (208-9).

Shelby Steele in the article "Existentialism in the Novels of Ayi Kwei Armah" has also related the floating sensations of the characters Roquentin and Baako to their indecisiveness. Steele argues, for instance, that the malaise of these characters stems from their inability to choose. On Roquentin, Steele writes:

> Roquentin is overly aware of life's immediate and minute details. They intrude into his consciousness with the same force as life and death issues. Because he only exists he, in effect, merges with the physical world. *He cannot assign relative importance to things because he cannot choose and so he cannot lift himself out of the overpowering present. Without an essence he is indistinguishable from the world around him. (Italics mine.)*[29]

Although Steele is correct in identifying the hypersensitivity of the character Roquentin, the analysis largely misses the mark. In failing to acknowledge Roquentin's decision to repudiate his vocation as historical biographer for that of a creative writer, Steele succeeds only in undermining the analysis by causal fallacy. That is, it may be argued that Roquentin, contrary to suffering from malaise because he lacks an essence, as Steele contends, suffers precisely because firstly, he recognizes that all roles are mere camouflages which prevent us from recognizing the superfluousness of our lives; secondly, that all attempts therefore to escape the fluid quality of the 'for-itself' will result in failure; and, thirdly, that his decision to devote himself exclusively to art is at best only a temporary reprieve from the anguish of the 'for-itself'. Steele, by failing to interpret the novel in light of its own conclusion and in light of Sartre's philosophical ideas, fails both to do justice to the thematic perspective of the novel and to the philosophical ideas of Sartre. Steele's analysis of the images of floating found in the literature may be considered more applicable to Baako Onipa of Armah's *Fragments,* but here again some qualification should be noted, since the effect or sensation of floating stems both from the character's indecisiveness and from the paralyzing effect of *the Look* of the Other which serves to reduce him to an 'in-itself'.

Baako's identification with the object world or with the 'in-itself' is first found in the chapter "Edin," which is narrated from the viewpoint of Juana, a Puerto Rican psychiatrist now transplanted in Ghana, who serves as a filtering consciousness of the novel. During one of her periodic escapes to the country to relieve the overwhelming sense of failure which comes from the unremitting and often futile treatment of mental patients, society's casualties, she comes across a group of men intently encircling a rabid dog who is lying on the warm pavement in the middle of the road. Of particular interest to her, though, is a man with a swollen scrotum whose sexual deformity urges him to be the first to murder the diseased animal.[30]

When the deformed man succeeds in murdering the animal, experiencing at the moment of his triumph a burst of energy which releases "the drip of life" that "had stayed locked up and poisoned the masculinity of his days," the implications are clear: impotent society in the form of the sexual cripple must sacrifice the life of a diseased but otherwise powerless animal for the realization of its own perverted aims. And that Baako, an artist and been-to, is conceived by Armah as the fictional equivalent of the rabid animal is clear from the various canine associations which punctuate the novel and which mark Baako's eventual descent into insanity.

In the chapter "Akwaaba," for example, after Baako's unannounced return to Ghana following an aborted one-week lay-over in Paris, he takes overnight lodgings in the hotel Avenida where he encounters a lean, wounded dog whose mournful howlings throughout the night serve as a futuristic omen.[31]

Later in the chapter "Awo," after Baako has been stymied by the bureaucracy at Ghanavision where he has gone to get a job as scriptwriter, he turns for help to his former schoolmaster Ocran who, in turn, takes him to see a personal friend, the Principal Secretary, who promises to talk things over with a club member, Quarcoo, "the one who makes decisions at the C.S.C. [Civil Service Commission]." Although Baako is instructed by the Principal Secretary to report to work the following day and is promised the sum of three weeks' pay for the time he has lost, the complacency of the system and his forced compromise have had a sullying effect. Following their departure, Ocran cannot contain his disgust and rage at a system which operates solely through solicitation and bribery and drives "like a drunken man," subsequently hitting and wounding a dog that has been attempting to cross the road.[32]

Finally, in the chapter entitled "Dam," the association of Baako with the rabid animal is driven home. Almost a year after his return, Baako suffers a relapse which is accompanied by weakness, fever, and a strange lucidity that leads to compulsive writing in his notebooks. The family members, believing him to be insane, attempt to fob him off as an asylum inmate under the pretext of affording him rest and recuperation. Baako, recognizing the deception, is able, at the last minute, to escape; however, in their second attempt to have him institutionalized, Baako is not successful. He is bound, hand and foot like the rabid animal in chapter two, and carted off to the Asylum, the canine images and those of nausea, vomit, and floating which have preceded his capture culminating to signal his demise by family and society who have petrified him into the object-world of the 'in-itself'.[33]

The scenes which contain both canine images and images of the viscous[34] are important to the existential themes in *Fragments* because they reflect, on the one hand, the character's victimization by the Other, in the form of family and society, who view him as a failure as a been-to, and, on the other, the character's subsequent pattern of self-recrimination at being unable to live up to society's prescribed image of himself as a been-to. The latter, the self-flagellation described by Brombart as typical of the Sartrean hero, is likewise reflected in Armah's depiction of Baako in *Fragments* and in the character's own description of the intellectual in a television treatment as an impotent.[35]

Similarly, Simone de Beauvoir's ambivalence toward the intellectual is evidenced in the short story "The Age of Discretion." Philippe, much to the dismay of his parents, one of whom is a university professor and writer, and the other, a respected scientist, makes the decision to quit his teaching post and abandon his research in order to join the Ministry of Culture. His decision, according to his wife, Irène, who defends his choice, is not a question of money, but rather of "being in the swim."[36]

On "the intellectual rapport" between Simone de Beauvoir and Jean-Paul Sartre, Simone de Beauvoir is reported by Deirdre Bair in her biography on Beauvoir as having said:

> . . . We began to work together [when] Sartre was twenty-three and I was twenty-one. Sartre was philosophically more creative than I, and it is in this respect that he had a great influence on me, because I didn't have a personal philosophy. I was interested in philosophical ideas and Sartre was creative and I quickly fell under the sway of his philosophy. . . . So philosophically I only had the role of a disciple, of someone who understood him well.[37]

Finally, the malaise of the intellectual hero, which manifests itself in sensations of floating, has been perceived by Victor Brombart as not only representative of the viscous but also of the perpetual sense of adolescence or immaturity which he finds descriptive of Mathieu Delarue, a bourgeois, pacifist, and conservative of Sartre's *The Age of Reason* who is noted for living out his life in "eternal parentheses." Mathieu abandons his mistress when he discovers that she is pregnant and seeks to remedy her condition by going to his lawyer-brother to seek money for a black market abortion. The contradiction he represents, though, is not lost on his brother who accuses him of both hypocrisy and deception. That is, according to Jacques, despite the fact that he eschews the bourgeois values associated with his family, he has no qualms about asking him for money. He chides him:

> "But I can't help feeling that with your ideas I should be rather chary of asking favors from a damned bourgeois. For I am a damned bourgeois," he added, laughing heartily. He went on, still laughing: "And what is worse, you, who despise the family, exploit our family ties to touch me for money. For, after all, you wouldn't apply to me if I wasn't your brother."[38]

Also, according to Jacques, although Mathieu envisages himself a pacifist, a defender of human life, his principles do not prevent him from resorting to "metaphysical murder" in order to solve a problem. And, finally, according to Jacques, despite his constant disavowal of marriage, his relationship with his mistress Marcelle, in its convenience and quiet domesticity, has rivaled marriage in everything but name. Jacques makes the observation:

> "You are a bourgeois by taste and temperament, and it's your temperament that's pushing you into marriage. For *you are married,* Mathieu," said he forcibly.
> "Oh yes, you are, only you pretend you aren't because you are possessed by theories. You have fallen into a habit of life with this young woman: you go to see her quietly four days a week and you spend the night with her. That has been going on for seven years, and there's no adventure left in it; you respect her, you feel obligations towards her, you don't want to leave her. And I'm quite sure that your sole object isn't pleasure. I even imagine that, broadly speaking, however vivid the pleasure may have been, it has by now begun to fade. In fact, I expect you sit beside her in the evening and tell her long stories about the events of the day and ask her advice in difficulties."[39]

Mathieu's problem, as Jacques sees it, is that he has refused to recognize his values for what they are--bourgeois--and has failed, on the pretext of a self-styled freedom, to take responsibility for his actions. In other words, as Jacques tells him, "'You have, however, reached the age of reason, my poor Mathieu. . . . But you try to dodge that fact too, you try to pretend you're younger than you are. Well--perhaps I'm doing you an injustice. Perhaps you haven't in fact reached the age of reason, it's really a moral age.'"[40]

Victor Brombart, taking his cue from the brother Jacques' assessment of Mathieu, has described the character in the work *The Intellectual Hero:*

> This thirty-four-year-old professor of philosophy, who tries to live out in petty-bourgeois comfort an adolescent resolve "to be free," appears to others as an "irresponsible aging student" living in eternal parentheses. . . . Throughout the

novel, the reactions of the other characters as well as his own relentless self-accusations point up his flaws. Mathieu knows that he is never *"dans le coup,"* that he has never truly bitten into life, that he has in fact led a toothless existence, *"une vie édentée."* Even his indignation against himself is empty rhetoric. His self-accusations are a form of self-indulgence.[41]

Consequently, the images of weightlessness and of floating which surround the character serve to disclose, according to Brombart, the insubstantiality of his existence which results from a life lacking firm commitment and cogent values. His old friend Brunet tells him:

> "You have spent thirty-five years cleaning yourself up, and the result is nil. . . . You live in a void, you have cut your bourgeois connections, you have no tie with the proletariat, you're adrift, you're an abstraction, a man who is not there. It can't be an amusing sort of life."[42]

This view by Brombart coincides strongly with the analysis already given of the been-to Baako of *Fragments* whose nausea and sensations of floating stem from his lack of resolve in the face of the Other as well as the one given of the exile Solo whose nausea stems from his bastardized European values.

The theme of cultural estrangement in *Why Are We So Blest?* has found genesis in the editorial in the Sunday *Times* entitled "Why Are We So Blest?." On the occasion of Thanksgiving which celebrates the blessings of America, Mike, a classmate of Modin's at Harvard, finds philosophical concordance with the columnist who depicts America as an Olympus, a Paradise, and "Christian Eden ignorant of the fall from Grace" and Americans as the blest. Those anomalies like Modin who have risen from the plains of mediocrity and who thus fall outside the analogy are categorized by Mike as "crossovers" (101).

That Solo, in many ways, parallels Modin is clear from the development of the novel. For example, like Modin, Solo has been Western-educated. Also like Modin, Solo has experienced the nihilating attraction of the black male for the white female. Finally, like Modin, Solo has attempted to redeem himself through African revolution, only to discover, even in revolution, a lack of saving grace.

Consistently, notwithstanding the overall tone of pessimism in the novel, revolutionary activity is offered by Armah as a means of escaping the malaise often afflicting the intellectual hero. Modin in *Why Are We So Blest?* rejects the principle of working within the system to disseminate anti-elite awareness, noting that it both ignores the mass of people and, paradoxically, seeks to effectuate change through the very medium of its destruction; however, the ideal of revolution he accepts for both its psychological and restorative value (222).

On the other hand, Jean-Paul's Sartre's faith in revolution may be gathered from his selection of images which contain in themselves judgements of value. Contrary to the intellectuals Mathieu and Hugo whose impotence is exposed in their obsessive self-contemplation, the Communist party leaders, Brunet and Hoederer in *The Age of Reason* and *Dirty Hands*, respectively, are described as solid characters whose density comes from firm values and revolutionary commitment. Of the two characters, however, Hoederer represents the consummate man of action because, unlike Brunet, whose self-assurance and rigid party discipline smack of an attitude of seriousness and bad faith, Hoederer refuses to be enslaved by political ideology. Guided by his own instincts, he breaks rank with the Communist party leaders in Ilyria who refuse to bargain with their enemies, goes out on a limb and makes a pact with the Fascist and nationalist forces of the government in order to ensure joint or corporate governorship following World War II, and dies for his principles before his unorthodox politics are given the stamp of approval by the officialdom in Moscow. Because he represents a man of authentic values and a person of good faith, the images surrounding him likewise convey impressions of authenticity and strength of character. Hugo, the intellectual and would-be assassin of Hoederer, speaks of the life-giving presence of Hoederer, or his ability to imbue objects with essence and character. To his wife, Jessica, he explains:

> HUGO: I don't know. [*A pause.*] It [the coffee pot] seems real when he touches it. [*He picks it up.*] Everything he touches seems real. He pours the coffee in the cups I drink. I watch him drinking and I feel that the taste of the coffee in his mouth is real. [*A pause.*] That it's the real flavor of coffee, real warmth, the real essence that is going to vanish. Only this will be left. [*He picks up the coffee pot.*][43]

The view of revolutionary activity as a means of escaping the malaise afflicting the intellectual hero has found genesis in Frantz Fanon, the late Algerian nationalist and psychiatrist who influenced the activist views of both Jean-Paul Sartre and Ayi Kwei Armah. This cross-cultural parallel between Sartre and Armah will be explored in the succeeding chapter, a parallel which serves to corroborate the existing philosophical associations between them.

1. Jean-Paul Sartre, *Existentialism and Humanism*, intro. and trans. Philip Mairet (London: Methuen, 1948), 34.

2. Ibid., 38.

3. Ibid., 40.

4. Ibid., 51.

5. Victor Brombart, *The Intellectual Hero: Studies in the French Novel 1880-1955* (Chicago: University of Chicago Press, 1964), 196.

6. Ibid., 188.

7. Jean-Paul Sartre, *Being and Nothingness: An Essay in Phenomenological Ontology*, intro. and trans. Hazel Barnes (New York: Philosophical Library, 1956), 153.

8. Ibid., 154.

9. Brombart, 190.

10. Ibid., 31.

11. Ibid., 181.

12. Simone de Beauvoir, *The Mandarins*, trans. Leonard M. Friedman (New York: W.W. Norton, 1991), 248.

13. Ibid., 401.

14. Ibid., 418.

15. Ayi Kwei Armah, *Why Are We So Blest?* (New York: Anchor Press, 1973), 68. All subsequent references to this edition will appear in the text.

16. O.S. Ogede, "Armah in Africa," *Ariel* 20, no. 4 (October 1990): 62.

17. Robert Fraser, *The Novels of Ayi Kwei Armah* (London: Heinemann, 1980), 50-51.

18. Ayi Kwei Armah, "A Mystification: African Independence Revalued," *Pan-African Journal* 2, no. 2 (spring 1969): 146.

19. George Lamming, Seminar on "Colonialism, Nationalism, and Identity in Caribbean Literature," Caribbean Writers Summer Institute, University of Miami, 1994.

20. George Lamming, introduction, *In the Castle of My Skin*, by George Lamming (New York: Schocken Books, 1983), xiv.

21. Ibid., 17.

22. Ayi Kwei Armah, *The Beautyful Ones Are Not Yet Born* (New York: Houghton Mifflin, 1968), 87.

23. Sartre, *Being and Nothingness*, 504.

24. Jean-Paul Sartre, *Existential Psychoanalysis*, intro. and trans. Hazel Barnes (New York: Philosophical Library, 1953), 196-97.

25. Jean-Paul Sartre, *The Age of Reason*, trans. Eric Sutton (New York: Alfred A. Knopf, 1947), 109.

26. Sartre, *Existential Psychoanalysis*, 133.

27. Jean-Paul Sartre, *Nausea*, trans. Lloyd Alexander (New York: New Directions, 1964), 134.

28. Alfred Stern, *Sartre: His Philosophy and Existential Psychoanalysis*, 2nd ed., rev. and enl. (New York: Delacorte Press, 1967), 195-96.

29. Shelby Steele, "Existentialism in the Novels of Ayi Kwei Armah," *Obsidian: Black Literature in Review* 3 (spring 1977): 11.

30. Ayi Kwei Armah, *Fragments* (New York: Collier Books, 1969), 36.

31. Ibid., 98-99.

32. Ibid., 126.

33. Ibid., 244-45.

34. Ibid., 228-29.

35. Ibid., 215.

36. Simone de Beauvoir, "The Age of Discretion," in *The Woman Destroyed*, trans. Patrick O'Brian (New York: G.P. Putnam's Sons, 1969), 27.

37. Deirdre Bair, *Simone de Beauvoir: A Biography* (New York: Summit, 1990), 143.

38. Sartre, *The Age of Reason*, 131.

39. Ibid., 136-37.

40. Ibid., 138.

41. Brombart, 183.

42. Sartre, *The Age of Reason,* 152-53.

43. Jean-Paul Sartre, *Dirty Hands,* in *No Exit and Three Other Plays* (New York: Knopf, 1955), 187.

Chapter 5

Revolution Versus Revolt

Germaine Brée in her comparative work, *Camus and Sartre: Crisis and Commitment*, includes Frantz Fanon among Sartre's list of heroes. According to Brée, Fanon exemplifies Sartre's theory of "praxis," the successful leap from theory into violent action. She writes:

> Sartre's formulation of his doctrine of commitment was a phase in the development of his enterprise. He set two goals for the writer—to unveil—disclose to his readers the developing patterns of the social world as seen through the eyes of the least favored among men; and, personally, joining action to thought, to close the gap between knowledge and practice. Both these aims assume the priority of acquiring knowledge in what Sartre now called "praxis," whether in the practice of writing or of life. . . .
> It was the ambiguous use he made of the word "action" which created a good deal of confusion, for a while reflecting his own nostalgia as an intellectual. Sartre has his roster of heroes—Castro, Lumumba, Fanon. Although since the fifties he has often specified that action, for the writer, can only be intellectual in kind, his fictional work, more specifically his plays, at one level are imaginary enactments of a lifelong dream of heroic participation in human affairs.[1]

By all accounts, Fanon expressed a similar high regard for Jean-Paul Sartre. In the biography *Sartre: A Life*, Solal reports on the 1960 meeting in Tunis between Fanon and emissaries of *Les Temps modernes* and the emissary Claude Lanzmann's account of the meeting:

> "[Fanon] had already read the *Critique of Dialectical Reason*, and he spoke to us about the illumination provided by certain models from the heart of the country, paragons of self-abnegation, sacrifice, and dedication. His need to communicate was immense; he wanted, above all, to convince us that the 'heart of Algeria' had become pure freedom, free of all prejudice. He told us that Sartre was a god."[2]

Axel Madsen, in his biography *Hearts and Minds: The Common Journey of Simone de Beauvoir and Jean-Paul Sartre,* gives the following account of a meeting between Frantz Fanon and Jean-Paul Sartre:

> On his way to cobalt treatment in northern Italy . . . , Fanon met Sartre and Simone for lunch in Rome. He was feverish and predicted a French invasion of Tunisia within the next forty-eight hours. When Simone broke off the conversation at 2 A.M. the following morning, politely insisting that Sartre needed rest, Fanon was outraged. No one in the provisional government slept more than a few hours, himself included. "I'd give twenty thousand francs a day to be able to talk to Sartre from morning to night for two weeks," Fanon later told Lanzmann. For three more days, they carried on their marathon talks and when Fanon came back through Rome after his cobalt treatment they talked another day.[3]

Brée, Solal, and Madsen's link of the French existentialist Jean-Paul Sartre to the late Algerian psychiatrist is important for two reasons. In the first place, it provides a common ground for a comparison of the Ghanaian author Ayi Kwei Armah with Sartre, since Armah was likewise influenced by Fanon; and, in the second place, it provides a basis for contrasting Armah and, correspondingly, Sartre with Camus, since the doctrine of revolutionary violence as espoused by Fanon in *The Wretched of the Earth* and endorsed by Sartre was clearly at variance with the views of *la mesure* as proposed by Camus in the works "Neither Victims nor Executioners," *The Rebel,* and *The Just Assassins.*

The influence of Frantz Fanon on Ayi Kwei Armah has been well-documented. Gareth Griffiths in the article "Structure and Image in Kwei Armah's *The Beautyful Ones Are Not Yet Born*" has called attention to Armah's indebtedness to Fanon, noting particularly the figurative language in *The Beautyful Ones* which complements the prose style of Fanon in *The Wretched of the Earth.* Referring to the image of the man-child in *The Beautyful Ones* which coincides with Fanon's description of the post-independence bourgeois leadership, Griffiths uses this description to justify his view of *The Beautyful Ones* as being, in part, "fictionalized Fanon." Griffiths makes the comparison:

> Fanon's analysis is objective, detached. It operates with an intense concern, but from above the disillusion, probing the roots and causes. Armah as novelist has dramatised the experience of the people themselves, their own tangled and confused hopes and their feeling that, perhaps, such decline and such premature destruction of their dream is natural and inevitable. Throughout chapter six Armah dramatises by image and scene Fanon's analysis of bourgeois corruption and psychic disturbance. This is the view from beneath the corruption, on the receiving end of the ordure and filth which the leadership pour down on the shoulders of those who lifted them up.[4]

Along these same lines, William Walker in "Major Ghanaian Fiction in English: A Study of the Novels of Ayi Kwei Armah and Kofi Awoonor," has taken up the argument of Armah's literature as being, to some degree, "fictionalized Fanon," Walker even going so far as to declare that the novels by Armah correspond to the phases of the former colonial writers--the assimilation, the remembrance, and the fighting--as described by Fanon in *The Wretched of the Earth*. For example, Armah's second novel, *Fragments*, Walker finds exemplary of the "remembrance" phase as described by Fanon. In *The Wretched of the Earth* Fanon had described the second phase:

> In the second phase we find the native is disturbed; he decides to remember what he is. This period of creative work approximately corresponds to that immersion which we have just described. . . . Past happenings of the byegone days of his childhood will be brought up out of the depths of his memory; old legends will be reinterpreted in the light of a borrowed estheticism and a conception of the world which was discovered under other skies.[5]

Walker, in light of the above, therefore has maintained:

> *Fragments* is indicative of this "remembrance" phase. The protagonist seeks to re-enter a fragmented world which holds his roots, his lost culture and his only source of redemption. This quest, however, is doomed in advance since the distance between the two worlds has become too great and the return path is no longer clear, buried under too many years of alien influence.[6]

Armah's own respect and admiration for Fanon can be seen in the article "African Socialism: Utopian or Scientific?." Judging African leaders, i.e., Leopold Senghor and Kwame Nkrumah, by the standards of the Marxist ideal, Armah ultimately dismisses them as frauds who engage in popular slogans to mask their colonialist mentality while, on the other hand, he goes on to identify Fanon as the only true articulator of African socialism:

> The one theorist who has worked out consistent formulations concerning . . . a revolutionary restructuring of African society is Frantz Fanon. A practising revolutionary, Fanon made himself an African, but never labelled himself a socialist. Analyzing (mainly from his vantage point in Accra) the antics of the post-Independence African leadership, he insistently and emphatically refused to be taken in by all the show. He knew all along that all the slogans and all the pomp and all the torrents of words were at bottom only an illusionist's art, and he said so.[7]

Most assuredly, the influence of Fanon on Armah has been so great that it has led one critic to remark that Armah is "becoming himself too much of a programmatic writer, . . . [adhering] too closely to Fanon's normative perspective."[8] Such a criticism of the writer is borne out in his third novel, *Why Are We So Blest?*, which adopts almost wholesale the ideas of Fanon as contained in *Black Skin, White Masks* and *The Wretched of the Earth.*

One of the themes treated in *Black Skin, White Masks* is the annihilating effect of the colonizing process, which creates a form of neurosis that often leads one to appropriate and internalize assets heretofore denied one, a condition which Fanon subsequently labels *affective erethism:* "A bilateral process, an attempt to acquire--by internalizing them--assets that were originally prohibited. . . ."[9] Symptomatic of this neurosis, which is founded upon an obsession with whiteness, are the exaggerated preference for European languages over one's native dialect and the neurotic pursuit of a white sexual partner, both of which represent, according to Fanon, a denial of one's blackness and, conversely, an assimilation of whiteness. Fanon has explained the psychology of the black male apropos the white female:

> Out of the blackest part of my soul, across the zebra striping of my mind, surges this desire to be suddenly *white.*
> I wish to be acknowledged not as black but as *white.*
> Now . . . who but a white woman can do this for me? By loving me she proves that I am worthy of white love. I am loved like a white man.
> I am a white man.
> Her love takes me onto the noble road that leads to total realization. . . .
> I marry white culture, white beauty, white whiteness.[10]

In Ayi Kwei Armah's *Why Are We So Blest?* one finds illustration of the destructive impulse characteristic of the male psyche as described by Fanon in *Black Skin, White Masks.* The African intellectual, Modin Dofu, suicidal because he has become an *assimilado,* becomes involved in futile relationships with white women in order to hasten his own destruction. One critic has observed: "The real journey that the author deals with . . . is an uneasy one taken by Modin, a young African intellectual, in and out of the peripheries of revolutionary involvement. Modin is a young man inspired not by hope but by a death wish."[11]

The motivation for Modin's suicidal tendencies stems from the historically meaningful term "factor," a term which in the context of the novel becomes identified with treason. It is noted that the factor functioned as an important intermediary in the trafficking of African slaves to the Europeans.[12] In similar fashion, Modin's Western education, financed by American scholarships, has entailed a similar compromise and has rendered him a double exile. According to Simon Gikandi:

> Modin goes to study in America, ostensibly to help his people 'develop', but what is supposed to be a process of uplifting becomes his spiritual death. He becomes

the victim of a social structure which is anti-African in its design, yet pays him to become a willing victim in a cycle of self-annihilation. [13]

Like the historical factor whose betrayal of his country and its people has been for purely self-serving purposes, Modin considers himself a modern-day Judas since his Western education has amounted to a black market trade-off (160-61). Armah links the Western education of the African elite to "neo-colonial accommodation in post-independence regimes to imperialism." According to Spencer:

In this novel *[Why Are We So Blest?]* he uses his character's experiences to reveal the socio-cultural and political factors which account for the neo-colonial accommodation in post-independence regimes to imperialism. He does this by focusing on the condition of Third World elites, in particular intellectuals who have received a Western education, for it is this group who inevitably hold positions of leadership within the liberation movements and later in the new nationalist governments and who as a result are in control of their nation's destiny. [14]

Ayi Kwei Armah considers "the idea of independence" specious, precisely because of the symbiotic relationship that has existed historically between the African and the European economies. In the article "A Mystification: African Independence Revalued," he has written that during the period of overt slavery,

Most of the business end of the system was left to a tellingly effective network of agents and local factors who stored and traded slaves, middlemen who peddled incentives manufactured in the European metropole or its American extension, and African chiefs, leaders, dignitaries . . . who produced the necessary disintegration, hence slaves, in their eagerness to acquire these incentives and thus aggrandize themselves. The point to note here is that most of the actual work needed to decimate the continent's human resources was done *in place* by Africans—leaders and chiefs being in the vanguard. So that an assessment that does not focus on the exocenter, the metropole also but concentrates on Africa would be misleading, presenting as it would the semblance of a series of independent, self-acting societies, when in fact the reality was that a subordinate subsystem was being torn apart in Africa to nourish and entertain a dominant metropole. [15]

One result of factorship is guilt. Modin realizes that the scholarships which finance his education are "blood money" intended to preserve the colonialist mentality and to keep the African peoples subject. In the words of O.S. Ogede:

What Solo and Modin, therefore, have in common with all the people like them who are products of Western education is their membership in a select group that, by training, are rendered incapable of participating in the struggle for the liberation of their people, an essentially proletarian struggle. The crises of identity that afflict the characters is a corollary to the guilt that comprises the self-inadequacy felt by educated Africans. [16]

Another result of factorship is alienation in the sense that elitism, while making Modin a traitor in one culture, has made him virtually a token in another. Such estrangement brought on by tokenism may be perceived in Modin's conversation with Oppenhardt, one of his benefactors at Harvard. Oppenhardt considers Modin an anomaly, "a most unusually intelligent African," and refers to him, condescendingly, as "boy." Subsequently, the knowledge that he is trapped between two worlds--attracted to both, accepted in neither--combined with the abiding loneliness which attends this alienation, leads ultimately to his destructive affairs with white women.

Modin is first taken in by the nymphomaniac wife of a middle-aged professor, Mrs. Jefferson, who uses him as a cure-all for her sexual ailment. Attracted to Modin because she naively believes in the stereotypical myth of the black man's sexual prowess, she quickly reveals herself for what she is--a human predator. Not only is she directly responsible for bringing Modin near death, for example, her husband discovers the two of them making love in the garden of his home and quickly dispatches Modin to the hospital with multiple dagger wounds, but she, characteristically, discards him after he is of no further use to her. After her ill-fated affair with Modin, she returns to improved marital relations with her husband, rejuvenated now by sexual fantasies of Modin, leaving Modin, as it were, to lick his own wounds. Naita, a young black secretary who had once befriended Modin, had warned him of his ultimate victimization (134).

Ironically, however, Modin's own realization of the true nature of these women comes too late. That is, only after his confinement to the hospital does he begin to recognize the self-destructive pattern of his relationships with white women, that he had been just "another rare creature, an African vehicle to help them reach the strange destinations of their souls" (167), despite all his rationalizations to the contrary. This knowledge, however, does not prevent him from being taken in by the feigned sincerity of another white liberal named Aimée Reitsch.

Aimée Reitsch, like Mrs. Jefferson, is described as a bourgeois liberal who is attracted to Africa and, by extension, to Africans because she craves the exotic and the forbidden. In her journal, for instance, her life gives the impression of being an endless search for fire and passion to counteract her gnawing sense of frigidity. She is dissatisfied with her life at Radcliffe and signs up for an African summer because she feels "if there is fire left anywhere that should be the place" (143). Subsequently, when Modin becomes involved with Aimée soon after the near-fatal relationship with Mrs. Jefferson, he knows the score. He knows that, like the protagonist in Ralph Ellison's *Invisible Man* who has to contend with white women who view him as "a domesticated rapist," he is a non-person, merely an instrument to be used by white women to realize their sexual fantasies. The warning signs against such an involvement were everywhere. As a newly-arrived student at Harvard, Modin had seen the dangers of assimilation in the educator Dr. Earl Lynch. Portrayed as a ludicrous character who has been decidedly brainwashed "to desire all flesh that is white," Dr. Lynch also has been guilty of the bad faith of interpreting his neurosis as some kind of insurrectionary act (163).

Moreover, Modin had been made aware through Aimée herself of the perverse nature of their relationship. In a moment of passion, Aimée had made it clear that her responses to Modin were predicated on fantasy, on whether she could sustain the illusion of Modin as the slave boy Mwangi caught up in a web of deceit, desire and danger manipulated by her and her settler husband (199). Nonetheless, the admission by Aimée that their relationship has been nothing but a lie is but confirmation of what others had suspected or known all along. An unnamed Afro-American had foreseen that Modin would become a victim of Aimée's neurotic lust and had warned him against involvement (200).

Not surprisingly then, in view of the above, Modin's relationship with Aimée ends tragically. The couple, experiencing growing dissatisfaction with their respective pursuits at Harvard and at Radcliffe, decide to engage their energies towards the constructive end of African revolution. They set off to Congheria, thinly-disguised Algeria, "the stamping ground of revolutionaries of all shades of persuasion."[17] To the revolutionaries at the Bureau of the People's Union of Congheria, however, they are a mockingly absurd couple--an African who wishes to engage in African revolution while accompanied by "the American child of the tribe of death" (230). They therefore seek to discourage the couple by putting them through interminable delays. They are instructed to fill forms and to return in two weeks, then another two weeks, and so on indefinitely until the couple, rather than give in to defeat, decide to make their way across the desert in order "to enter the maquis by the back door."[18] Subsequently, it is here in the midst of the Sahara desert that a band of French marauders, angered by the sight of the inter-racial couple, rape Aimée and proceed to castrate the defenseless Modin, leaving him alone to die in the desert. The frightened Aimée, forcibly stripped of all her disguises, decides then to return to America and to her bourgeois money; but before she leaves Congheria, she goes to reclaim the notebooks which she had trustingly left in the hands of Solo Nkonam, a Portuguese-educated Ghanaian, and, like Modin, a failed revolutionary. Notably, it is during one of their brief last encounters that Aimée, accompanied by the white mistress of one of the bureaucrats at the Bureau of the People's Union of Congheria, is seen in her most predatory state (269).

Some critics have voiced concern over the obvious stereotyping of the characters in *Why Are We So Blest?* which is part and parcel of the anti-Western slant of the novel. For example, the characters are placed into irreconcilable camps of black and white with the white characters all too often identified as the destructive agents; the black(s) all too often identified as victim(s). Robert Fraser, in his review of the novel, has assessed the novel's characterization:

> Armah is not humanly affected by his white characters since he is interested only to mark them out as agents of destruction. Thus Aimée, for instance, is almost an allegorical figure: she exists simply to demonstrate the rapacious main chord of her personality. The other white characters are distinctly shadowy, flitting around Dofu and torturing his spirit: they have no other function.[19]

Similarly, William Walker has accused Armah of "belabouring the evils of racism without matching such thoroughness with corresponding characterization." The result, then, as Walker sees it, is that "the thesis comes through loud and clear, but the novel never catches hold of its reader as it might if the characters were brought to life."[20]

By the same token, Norman Albritton Spencer describes Aimée as "grotesque" and her characterization emblematic of the lack of authorial distance between the writer and his subject:

> The portrayal of Aimée is in most instances grotesque and disturbing because it is obviously a reflection of the author's distorted rage at the West. There is not enough authorial distance, and for this reason the reader is subjected to a rough and unrealistic image of the author's undigested emotional response.[21]

Undoubtedly, the novel lacks credibility, since fictional realism is sacrificed to social symbolism. The characters are forced to assume roles which, in turn, make them cardboard characters rather than real-life personalities. An example of this blatant stereotyping is found in the aforementioned character Aimée, who is portrayed throughout the novel as both frigid and destructive.

An example of Aimée's frigidity is found near the end of the novel. In one of his diary entries Modin describes the couple's hopeless attempt to cross the Sahara desert in order to make direct contact with the maquis. The crossing is made in December in the midst of frigid temperatures; however, unlike Modin whose expiration is symbolized by the cold, Aimée is described as remarkably unaffected (280).

Earlier, Modin had recalled the experiment at the Psycho Lab, where he often volunteered himself as subject, following his break with Oppenhardt and the members of the Committee, in order to supplement a dwindling income. As part of the experiment electric shocks were administered to the body in varying degrees of intensity in order to determine the subjects' "threshold of tolerance for pain." The subjects averaged, respectively, 4.7, 5.0, 4.9, 5.1, etc.; however, Aimée, who later admitted that she had volunteered herself as subject because she wanted to feel, had registered an astounding 11.2 and 13.8 on two consecutive readings. The point to be drawn from this is clear. Aimée is not only frigid, but her masochistic nature will lead to the death and destruction of Modin. One of the experimenters, Joel, as though recognizing the destructive capacity of Aimée, through a veiled look of complicity, had tried to warn Modin against sexual involvement with Aimée (171).

Given the development of the novel, its thematic intent is unmistakable. That is, picking up a strain which was begun in the previous novel, *Fragments*, on the alienation of the Western-educated African who returns home to find himself out of step with his society, Armah, as he has done in the short story "Yaw Manu's Charm," probes deeper in *Why Are We So Blest?* into the reasons for this alienation, ultimately justifying it as the result of the indoctrination created by Western influences. Nonetheless, to the extent that the alienation which Armah describes is not only externally imposed but, in addition, internally imposed, it coincides with the self-destructive neurosis which Fanon has described in *Black Skin, White Masks*. It coincides, as well, with the neurosis which Jean-Paul Sartre has discussed in *Being and Nothingness* under the heading of masochism.

The attitude of masochism Sartre has described in *Being and Nothingness* as the failure of love. In love one attempts to possess the freedom of the other, so that in the act of possession one can recapture all that was lost through the gaze of the Other. Through *The Look* of the Other, one was victimized. One was placed outside of oneself and hence violated by the unsympathetic gaze of the Other. However, through love one attempts to regain oneself, one's objectness for the Other. In brief, one attempts to become the foundation of one's being by having the image of oneself as an 'in-itself' reflected affirmatively in the eyes of the Other. Sartre goes on to explain:

> Whereas before being loved we were uneasy about that unjustified, unjustifiable protuberance which was our existence, whereas we felt ourselves "de trop," we now feel that our existence is taken up and willed even in its tiniest details by an absolute freedom which at the same time our existence conditions and which we ourselves will with our freedom. This is the basis for the joy of love when there is joy: we feel that our existence is justified.
>
> By the same token if the beloved can love us, he is wholly ready to be assimilated by our freedom; for this being-loved which we desire is already the ontological proof applied to our being-for-others. Our objective essence implies the

existence of the Other, and conversely it is the Other's freedom which founds our essence. If we could manage to interiorize the whole system, we should be our own foundation.[22]

However, in Sartre's view, the ideal of love is doomed to failure, principally because one cannot demand of the Other that he found one's being without the Other demanding the same thing of the beloved. In other words, to love is to want to be loved. Therefore, one cannot escape into objectness without being thrown back onto one's own free subjectivity. Sartre has written in *Being and Nothingness:*

> I demand that the Other love me and I do everything possible to realize my project; but if the Other loves me, he radically deceives me by his very love. I demanded of him that he should found my being as a privileged object by maintaining himself as pure subjectivity confronting me; and as soon as he loves me he experiences me as subject and is swallowed up in his objectivity confronting my subjectivity.[23]

The recognition of the destructibility of love may, therefore, lead to masochism. Since the beloved cannot succeed in realizing himself completely through the Other, he may then decide to forfeit his freedom, to make himself the willing object of the Other in order to avoid the dread anguish of the 'for-itself':

> The Other has referred me to my own unjustifiable subjectivity--either by himself or through others. This result can provoke a total despair and a new attempt to realize the identification of the Other and myself. Its ideal will then be the opposite of that which we have just described; instead of projecting the absorbing of the Other while preserving in him his otherness, I shall project causing myself to be absorbed by the Other and losing myself in his subjectivity in order to get rid of my own. This enterprise will be expressed concretely by the *masochistic* attitude.[24]

The character Paula of Simone de Beauvoir's *The Mandarins* is a case in point. She has sacrificed her singing career, freedom, and, ultimately, her sanity for the sake of "a great love" in order to avoid the anguish that devolves from the project of inventing herself. Henri pondered, "He had never been able to decide whether she really scorned fame or whether she was afraid of not being able to attain it." [25] However, masochism, like love, is, in principle, a failure. The masochist wants to become the instrument for the Other, but it is he who uses the Other toward the realization of his own ends. The masochist can never succeed in perceiving himself as an object. To himself, he remains a transcendence, locked within itself.

Simon Gikandi, in his work *Reading the African Novel,* considers the masochistic urge peculiar to Armah's characters, namely their self-righteous battle against certain defeat. Baako of *Fragments* is therefore regarded as emblematic in this regard:

Unlike Juana, Baako does not utilize the weapon of escape effectively; he seems to play up to those situations that oppress his inner being. For instance, he insists on taking up a job at the television station, although people who should know have warned him not to expect anything useful to happen there; he agrees to be the master of ceremonies at the premature outing of his sister's baby, even when he abhors the motive behind it. It is as if he confronts the most naked aspects of the oppressive culture to convince himself that he has indeed failed.[26]

On the other hand, the masochistic urge and the attendant bad faith of Modin in *Why Are We So Blest?* are implicated in the modishly apish appearance of the couple when they first visit the office of the UPC. In one of Solo's journal entries he recalls seeing the couple for the very first time at the office of the UPC and remarking their almost complete lack of identity as a result of their assimilation (56).

Also, the masochistic urge of Modin has been discerned by the officials at the office of the UPC. Both Esteban Ngulo and Jorge Manuel draw the conclusion, based upon the couple's appearance, that Modin is unfit to join the struggle for independence, citing, collectively, the character's perverse motive; that is to say, he is on a death mission (255). K. Damodar Rao in his critical work provides the following insight into Modin's dysfunction:

Modin's views on communal well-being which he terms as the maquis, at the societal level, and on his own inadequacy to partake in that process, his isolation and death-bound journey are quite accurate in that they provide a fairly objective self-assessment. But the moment he sees Aimée he gets hypnotically anaesthetized and falters—at the cost of his individuality and ultimately his life.[27]

Edward Lobb in his article "Personal and Political Fate in Armah's *Why Are We So Blest?*" also remarks the suicidal nature of Modin:

The attempt to overcome it [his alienation] politically is at odds with the attempt to overcome it personally with Aimée. Modin is attempting to go in two directions at one, and realizes from the beginning that "the directions made available . . . within this arrangement are all suicidal" (p. 31). Esteban Ngulo, Manuel's secretary, likewise sees that Modin is "one of those intellectuals who wants to die" (p. 255). Modin's attempts to join forces with the rebels in Congheria is not an endorsement, on his part or Armah's, of revolutionary violence: it is a private choice of a way to die.[28]

Finally, Modin's masochism is forcefully represented in the symbol of his castration, which forms the culmination of his pattern of self-destructiveness. In graphic detail Armah describes the sexual torture of Modin by the French soldiers, forcibly aided by Aimée, and Aimée's neurotic and sadistic pleasure at the realization of her sexual fantasy of Modin as the slave boy Mwangi. And that Modin has deliberately willed his destruction at the hands of Aimée is patently clear from his notebook entries. After quitting Harvard, for a life of revolutionary engagement in newly-independent Algeria, Modin had written of confronting racism in the most blatant and deadly form. That is, surrounded by defeated French soldiers in the midst of the Sahara desert, Modin had experienced himself, from the vengeful and destructive looks of the French soldiers, as a would-be victim (275).

Because of such open displays of racial hostility by the French soldiers, Modin could no longer conveniently ignore the fact that Aimée is white and that she likewise carries within her the very seed of his destruction. More specifically, he could no longer ignore the congruity between Aimée and the Boston female photographed in a Boston newspaper who, after winning the trust and confidence of her male friend, had sadistically "cut off her man friend's testicles with a nail clipper, put them in her handbag, then tried to disappear southward, into the South American hinterland" (276).

Importantly, though, this masochistic urge identified in Modin is considered by Armah as common to all those who likewise have been so assimilated. Jorge Manuel, Foreign Minister of the Congherian Government, described also as being Portuguese-educated, is said to have a white, middle-aged mistress whose "love" Solo can only interpret as yet another manifestation of hate (229).

Further, Ndugu Pakansa, head of state of Kansa and European traveler, may be said to be guilty of this same destructive affectation. Such is shown when he refuses to cooperate with the Moja Moja revolutionaries by agreeing to espionage, principally because to do so would jeopardize the European interests so symbolized in his white mistress. Significantly, like Jorge Manuel's mistress, Pakansa's mistress is described too as having only her whiteness to recommend her. One of the emissaries describes her: "No matter how kind you wanted to be, you could not call that woman beautiful. She was not young. There was nothing in her face or in her motion that spoke of wisdom" (38).

Finally, even the narrator himself, the Portuguese-educated Solo Nkonam, describes himself as not immune to the ubiquitous and destructive attraction to the white woman. The sight of the inter-racial couple, Modin and Aimée, at the office of the UPC, for instance, only brought back to him unpleasant memories of his own suicidal tendencies as manifested by his European absorption. That is, Solo, believing himself in love, had proposed marriage to the Portuguese female Sylvia, only to be forced to recognize the bad faith of the relationship by the discriminatory presence of the Other in the form of white society. Solo recalls the destruction of their illusion of love by the interference from Sylvia's Portuguese friends, who had categorized their affair as a vile "sickness" (65).

In *Being and Nothingness* Jean-Paul Sartre had determined *the Look* of the Other as a second reason for the failure of love, since *the Look* of the Other, in its free and objective nature, belied the lovers' mutual attempt to make the other the "absolute by which the world comes into being."[29] That is, for themselves they may become the beloved's ultimate end and complete source of value; however, for an objective third, they become no more than mere objects in the world capable therefore of being transcended. According to Sartre, this is the true reason why lovers seek solitude: to preserve the illusion of their complete freedom and sovereignty. However, just as Sartre's eavesdropping spy experienced shame from an imaginary Other, the mere existence of the Other will serve to undermine, even in the lovers' complete solitude, their hopes of achieving an autonomous relationship free from the petrifying and, therefore, reductive gaze of the Other. Sartre notes in *Being and Nothingness* that

> Factual solitude (e.g., we are alone in my room) is by no means a theoretical solitude. Even if nobody sees us, we exist for *all* consciousnesses and we are conscious of existing for all. The result is that love as a fundamental mode of being-for-others holds in its being-for-others the seed of its own destruction.[30]

Exemplary of the destructibility of love by the Other is Sartre's own play *No Exit*. Joseph Garcin, a coward and war deserter, would feel himself vindicated if he could have the image of himself as "a tough" reflected affirmatively in the eyes of Estelle Rigault, a femme fatale and child murderer; however, Inez Serrano, a lesbian and die-hard sadist who competes with Garcin for the attention of Estelle, taunts Garcin for his cowardice and mocks their love-making as a charade, thus succeeding in driving a permanent wedge between them and ruining their chances of forming a deceptive partnership exclusive of her. She scorns their hopeless attempts at lovemaking:

> "I'm watching you, everybody's watching, I'm a crowd all by myself. Do you hear the crowd? Do you hear them muttering, Garcin? Mumbling and muttering. 'Coward! Coward! Coward! Coward!'--that's what they're saying. . . . It's no use trying to escape, I'll never let you go. What do you hope to get from her silly lips? Forgetfulness? But I shan't forget you, not I! 'It's I you must convince.' So come to me. I'm waiting. Come along, now. . . . Look how obedient he is, like a well-trained dog who comes when his mistress calls. You can't hold him, and you never will."[31]

The scene of the break-up between Solo and Sylvia in *Why Are We So Blest?* is therefore particularly important because it reveals, as Sartre had noted in *Being and Nothingness*, the destructibility of love by *the Look* and the judgement of the Other; it is also important because it reveals the bad faith of Solo and, correspondingly, of Modin in mistaking masochism for love (139).

Accordingly, the only way out of the vicious neurotic circle which has been one of the effects of colonialism was, in Fanon's view, revolutionary violence. Revolutionary violence, in Fanon's view, would not only return the indigenous population to the pre-colonialist structure, but would eradicate, by force, the Master-Slave mentality which had spawned psychic oppression. Fanon had defended violence in *The Wretched of the Earth:* "At the level of individuals, violence is a cleansing force. It frees the native from his inferiority complex and from his despair and inaction; it makes him fearless and restores his self-respect."[32]

Fanon's justification of revolutionary violence, Marxist in derivation since it subscribes to historical expediency, to the view that destructive or violent means may be sanctioned if the end is a just one, further extends the similarity between Jean-Paul Sartre and Ayi Kwei Armah, both of whom were supporters of Fanon and, likewise, sympathizers of Marxism. It negates, however, on these grounds, a parallel association of these writers with Albert Camus, a proponent of *la mesure* and, contrary to the above, an opponent of Marxism.

Ben Obumselu in his article "Marx, Politics and the African Novel" has broadened the interpretation of Armah's *The Beautyful Ones Are Not Yet Born* by reading it as Armah's expression of "the exploitation of the African proletariat." Justifying the interpretation from the article "African Socialism, Utopian or Scientific?" where Armah had successfully debunked nationalist leaders such as Senghor and Nkrumah on the basis of their backward-looking, self-serving and reactionary-type politics, Obumselu, in the article, goes on to discuss *The Beautyful Ones* as a mythic illustration of the failure of socialism. He has written:

> *The Beautyful Ones* is best read as myth. Its treatment of the corruption of power, of the contradictions inherent in the idea of the benevolent autocrat, of the oppression of social and political experience, as patterns which repeat themselves suggests that the operative imaginative form is that of myth.[33]

To further sustain his view of the novel as social myth, Obumselu argues the essential germ of the novel as contained in Armah's sketch, "An African Fable," where Armah had corrected the folkloric version of the knight errant and the damsel in distress by describing a situation of double rape: an elder warrior who rapes the damsel and a knight errant who rescues the damsel, only to become himself the rapist. According to Obumselu, the theme of betrayal as found in Armah's "An African Fable" corresponds closely to the political situation in contemporary

Ghana as described by Armah in *The Beautyful Ones.* Obumselu has made the parallel, subsequently concluding:

This is the story (in *The Beautyful Ones)* of Oyo, her mother and the fishing boats. It is important to notice that it is also the story of Nkrumah and the people of Ghana. Maanan who plays the damsel against Nkrumah's warrior appropriately ends in exhaustion and madness and is shown sifting the sands looking presumably for her lost illusions.[34]

Obumselu has attributed the Marxist parallels in the literature by Armah to the influence of Frantz Fanon, Marx's "foremost black exponent and adaptor," who, in Obumselu's view, has altered Marxism "to accommodate the subjective angle of a psychiatrist and a Sartrean existentialist, and . . . to accord with the first loyalties of the spokesman of the black revolution."[35] The particular influences of Fanon on Armah he thereupon notes as the "intensely paranoid" characters, whose psychological ailment often reflects a pervasive social ailment, and the viewpoint of the peasant classes as being "the truly revolutionary class in Africa." Reading Armah's article, "African Socialism: Utopian or Scientific?" as a "programme for the novel," *The Beautyful Ones,* Obumselu has observed:

Armah's point of view in the article taken as a whole has many elements deriving from Fanon, the most noticeable feature being the casual dismissal of the urban classes who are silently compared with the peasantry considered by Fanon, quite rightly, as the truly revolutionary class in Africa.[36]

Although it may be conceded alongside Obumselu that *The Beautyful Ones* is revolutionary literature in that the seeds of revolution are planted in a disgruntled lower-class clerk, who represents a growing and fundamental disquiet, Armah's third novel, *Why Are We So Blest?,* may be better termed revolutionary literature, since through his characters Armah not only denounces the Western influences, but issues a challenge to African peoples to take up arms against their mental shackles. The revolutionary perspective of the novel is reflected, in part, through Modin, who relates his reasons for wanting to join the maquis, namely, to restore an egalitarian social order (222).

However, the most cogent example of Ayi Kwei Armah's commitment to revolution appears to be contained in his fourth novel, *Two Thousand Seasons,* which continues in the vein of *Why Are We So Blest?* but which, to date, makes the strongest claims of spiritual renewal through revolution.

The revolutionary concept of the novel is encapsulated in a group of twenty initiates--eleven females and nine males--who, collectively, represent those indigenous and nationalist forces that have served

throughout African history to wrest a mean independence from
oppressive European forces. Identified with the regenerative and
cleansing nature of water, the members of the group symbolize the hope
for Africa's re-emergence through the destruction of malignant forces
opposed to "the way" and to reciprocity.[37]
According to Armah's "remembrance," the undoing of the African
peoples has been their indiscriminate generosity. When white
missionaries came from the sea seeking land, shelter, and a place to
practice their religion, the indigenous population treated them with all
the hospitality befitting guests, not foreseeing that those few amongst
them would turn predators against them. The price of such blind
acceptance has been the sentence of two thousand seasons, or one
hundred years, of oppression, as Anoa has prophesied.[38] Combined
with Anoa's prophecy has been also an appeal to "the way" and a call
for the destruction of those responsible for the rape of African soil and
the pillage of its people.[39]
Although Armah saves his most strident attacks for the predators who
are identified throughout the novel as the imperialists--the Arabs and the
Europeans--he shows no less contempt for the African heads of state and
their hangers-on he has designated "parasites." They are comprised of
opportunists similar to Joe Koomson in *The Beautyful Ones* and Jorge
Manuel in *Why Are We So Blest?* whose only ambition is "to place
themselves on their master's stool." The character Kamuzu is described
as one of them. A divided soul whose enmity against the royals makes
him conspire with the rebels to seize the stone castle, Kamuzu's
"poverty of vision" is revealed from his corrupt ulterior motives. That
is, Kamuzu aids and abets the rebels in the seizure of the castle and the
murder of the Europeans only because he wants to get even with some
African princes who have cheated him out of his agreed-upon share of
the profits from their slavedealing; however, once ensconced there in the
castle, he betrays his true ambition, "to become a copy of the chief of
the white destroyers we had found in this place, the one they had called
the governor," by striving to protect the spoils of the castle for himself:
the governor's mistress, servants, and clothing.[40]
Characteristically, he also attempts to betray the rebels, but, in his
foolhardiness, is himself betrayed. That is, he makes a pact with "the
destroyers" which is designed in the end to drive the rebels out of the
stone palace and to keep Kamuzu supreme there, "a black copy of the
head white destroyer."[41] The rebels, however, wary of Kamuzu,
discover his plan of deception and arrange to transfer the military
supplies from the castle before the planned ambush. They take care,
however, before their departure, to ignite the remaining gunpowder kept
locked in the stores beneath the castle, thus destroying the castle and

sealing Kamuzu's fate. Kamuzu, for all his trouble, is hanged by the Europeans for his bungling attempts at power-grabbing and for his ineptitude at playing both sides of the fence: "His crime, the new interpreter the destroyers had found was told to say, was something called presumption."[42] For those like Kamuzu it is given the reader to understand that destruction is their only fitting reward. Armah describes the mission of the rebels as being, in part, "the halting of this white destruction turned against us" by "the removal of parasites whose greed welcomes destruction's white empire."[43]

Despite the consistent identification of the initiates with aggression and violence, Armah is careful not to condone gratuitous violence. Identifying the vulture, the bird that lives off carrion but never kills a living thing, as the symbol of the group, violence in the framework of the novel represents no more than a catharsis aimed at the purging of destructive forces opposed to the liberation of Africa. In the words of Kofi Anyidoho:

> To the 'brainless' and to men of 'fractured vision' the vulture is an object of scorn, but to the people of 'the way' the vulture's basic affinity is obvious and deserving of respect: its life, like theirs, is guided by a moral law, that no creature may satisfy its life's needs by depriving others of theirs.[44]

The conception for the novel has found inspiration in the Algerian psychiatrist Frantz Fanon's *The Wretched of the Earth*. In *The Wretched of the Earth* Fanon has spoken of violence as a creative force identifiable with self-realization and autonomy:

> We have said that the native's violence unifies the people. By its very structure, colonialism is separatist and regionalist. Colonialism does not simply state the existence of tribes; it also reinforces it and separates them. The colonial system encourages chieftaincies and keeps alive the old Marabout confraternities. Violence is in action all-inclusive and national. It follows that it is closely involved in the liquidation of regionalism and of tribalism. Thus the national parties show no pity at all toward the caids and the customary chiefs. Their destruction is the preliminary to the unification of the people.[45]

Similarly, in *Two Thousand Seasons* Armah has defended violence as a necessary means to an end. That is, differentiating between violence for its own sake and violence posited toward the constructive end of African revolution, Armah upholds violence based exclusively on the positive effects of nationalism.[46]

Such a pragmatic view of violence likewise has been endorsed by Jean-Paul Sartre, who wrote the Preface to Fanon's *The Wretched of the Earth*. Observing that violence has been the legacy of the Europeans to the colonized, Sartre not only credits violence for the psychic liberation of those whose history has been scarred by violence, but he also utilizes the opportunity to criticize the left-wing intellectuals and believers in non-violence for their convenient form of duplicity. On the latter he has written in the Preface to *The Wretched of the Earth:*

> A fine sight they are too, the believers in non-violence, saying that they are neither executioners nor victims. Very well then; if you're not victims when the government which you've voted for, when the army in which your younger brothers are serving without hesitation or remorse have undertaken race murder, you are, without a shadow of doubt, executioners. And if you choose to be victims and to risk being put in prison for a day or two, you are simply choosing to pull your irons out of the fire. But you will not be able to pull them out; they'll have to stay there till the end. Try to understand this at any rate: if violence began this very evening and if exploitation and oppression had never existed on the earth, perhaps the slogans of non-violence might end the quarrel. But if the whole regime, even your non-violent ideas, are conditioned by a thousand-year-old oppression, your passivity serves only to place you in the ranks of the oppressors.[47]

The target of the above commentary was Albert Camus's article "Neither Victims nor Executioners." In the article, Camus had accused the adherents of Marxism of sacrificing human lives for a Utopian ideal which, in its implacable logic, ended up perverting its original aims. He had written:

> In the Marxian perspective, a hundred thousand corpses are nothing if they are the price of the happiness of hundreds of millions of men. But the sure death of millions of men for the hypothetical happiness of the survivors seems too high a price to pay. The dizzy rate at which weapons have evolved, a historical fact ignored by Marx, forces us to raise anew the whole question of means and ends. And in this instance, the means can leave us little doubt about the end. Whatever the desired end, however lofty and necessary, whether happiness or justice or liberty—the means employed to attain it represent so enormous a risk and are so disproportionate to the slender hopes of success, that in all sober objectivity, we must refuse to run this risk.[48]

As a humanist, Camus was opposed to what he had referred to in "Neither Victims nor Executioners" as "legitimized murder." Camus recognized a decency, a common value in man which he could not see betrayed or mutilated for such abstract notions as progress or history; hence, Camus's preference for revolt which, unlike revolution, did not betray its original conception but, instead, respected the limits which had given it utterance. He was later to distinguish in *The Rebel* between rebellion and revolution:

> Rebellion, in its original authenticity, does not justify any purely historical concept. Rebellion's demand is unity; historical revolution's demand is totality. The former starts from a negative supported by an affirmative, the latter from absolute negation and is condemned to every aspect of slavery in order to fabricate an affirmative that

is dismissed until the end of time. One is creative, the other nihilist. The first is
dedicated to creation so as to exist more and more completely; the second is forced
to produce results in order to negate more and more completely.[49]

The upshot of Camus's treatment of the question of means and ends
is that his subsequent theory of *la mesure* became one of the governing
principles for his stand on real-life issues. More specifically, his views
on revolt and revolution ultimately conditioned his response to the
question of Algerian independence, which set in sharp relief his
differences with the writers Sartre, Fanon, and Armah. In the work
Resistance, Rebellion, and Death, where Camus has written at length on
the question of Algeria's independence, it is given the reader to
understand that Camus disapproved of full autonomy both because of
the likely expulsion of the French citizens in Algeria as a result of
national independence, and because of the torture and persecution of the
French citizens in Algeria by the Front for National Liberation. For
example, Camus refused to recognize the Front for National Liberation,
condemning its leaders as "the most relentless of the insurrection," and
called for an end to the terrorist activity through government
intervention. Recalling the 1905 terrorists in his own play *The Just
Assassins*, who, in Camus's view, represented "the highest peak of
revolutionary momentum," since the comrades of the Revolutionary
Socialist Party "triumphed over nihilism,"[50] by refusing to base
revolution on injustice, deceit, and gratuitous murder, Camus had issued
the following challenge:

> To be both useful and equitable, we must condemn with equal force and in no
> uncertain terms the terrorism applied by the F.L.N. to French civilians and indeed,
> to an even greater degree, to Arab civilians. Such terrorism is a crime that can be
> neither excused nor allowed to develop. Under the form it has assumed, no
> revolutionary movement has ever accepted it, and the Russian terrorists in 1905, for
> instance, would have died (they proved this statement) rather than stoop to it. It
> would be impossible to transform an awareness of the injustices imposed on the
> Arab population into a systematic indulgence toward those who indiscriminately
> slaughter Arab and French civilians without regard for age or sex.[51]

The perversion of revolution to which Camus was staunchly opposed
is cogently represented in Nigerian author Buchi Emecheta's *Destination
Biafra*.[52] The author equates the Nigerian-Biafran conflict to genocide
orchestrated by the British to control the oil-rich fields of Nigeria and
effectuated by the two warring generals, Saka Momoh, a Northern Tiv,
and Chijioke Abosi, an Eastern Igbo, who transmute the conflict into an
opportunity to settle personal scores. *Destination Biafra* therefore
dramatizes the harm repudiated by Camus when principle becomes
subverted by either economic or militaristic expediency.

On the other hand, for Fanon who in *The Wretched of the Earth* had described violence as the legacy of the colonial system, the advocacy of pacification by Europeans was but to play a double game, to seek to disarm the colonized of their most powerful weapon. On violence, Fanon had written:

> The existence of an armed struggle shows that the people are decided to trust to violent methods only. He of whom *they* [the colonialists] have never stopped saying that the only language he understands is that of force, decides to give utterance by force. In fact, as always, the settler has shown him the way he should take if he is to become free. The argument the native chooses has been furnished by the settler, and by an ironic turning of the tables it is the native who now affirms that the colonialist understands nothing but force.[53]

Annie Cohen-Solal has summarized in *Sartre: A Life* the ideological differences separating Camus and Sartre, based largely on their response to Stalinism or Marxism:

> For Camus, the denunciation of the various incarnations of Stalinism should have gone unhesitatingly to the very bottom of all its crimes. Sartre was a partisan of truth, but with an eye to extenuating circumstances. Camus believed in the equation of Stalinism and fascism. Sartre was trying, in a complex and sophisticated way, to find a possible compromise between ethics and politics. Camus was trying to conceptualize the same premises but in a much more antagonistic fashion. Sartre was opting for ethical pragmatism, Camus, more radically, for the refusal of all violence no matter what its origins and premises. Their perspectives concerning the role of ethics in politics were quite different. Sartre looked for the moral perspective in politics, but he also tried to reconcile it to the dimension of strategic choices . . .; Camus, instead, entrenched himself behind his principles and moral strictures, and refused to bow to political polemics. Sartre tried to cope with reality while Camus invoked his ethical principles; no dialogue was possible between them.[54]

John Cruickshank, in a similar vein, has referred to the dissension between Sartre and Camus as "the fundamental debate of our time--the argument between Marxism and the non-Marxist left."[55] Such a statement might apply also, with qualification, to Frantz Fanon, Ayi Kwei Armah, and Albert Camus respectively. Although the responses of Fanon and Armah to revolution were conditioned by their own countries' successful bid for independence, they were conditioned no less by their own Marxist inclinations. Ayi Kwei Armah in the article "African Socialism: Utopian or Scientific?" has noted that Marxism is "the most spectacularly successful counter to Western capitalist thought," implicitly due to its "archetypal dream of liberation" for "the dispossessed working man."[56]

On the other hand, Sartre's Marxist affinities have become well-known. For years a staunch critic of the Communist party for its doctrinaire politics and its subjugation of the human element to determinism, Sartre, however, in later years came to view Marxism as "the unsurpassable philosophy" of our time, since the economic and historical conditions which prompted it remain alive.[57] In 1960 with the publication of *Critique of Dialectical Reason*, Sartre announced the future abdication of existentialism in favor of Marxism by noting its *raison d'être* would soon be extinct: "From the day on which Marxist research will take the human dimension (that is to say, the existential project) as the foundation of anthropological knowledge, Existentialism will no longer have any reason for being."[58] However, even prior to the publication of *Critique of Dialectical Reason*, Sartre's growing attraction to Marxist views was apparent, notably in the political play *Dirty Hands*, which comparable to both Fanon's *The Wretched of the Earth* and Armah's *Why Are We So Blest?* and *Two Thousand Seasons*, justifies violence for political ends.

To illustrate, Hoederer, General Secretary of the Communist party targeted for assassination for allegedly selling out the party to the enemy, is not above the means of violence, compromise, and deceit if they will enable him to realize the goal of the party--political power. To that end, he will resort to subterfuge by surreptitiously negotiating with the enemy forces of the government of Ilyria in order to ensure corporate governorship following the war, even at the expense of being labeled a traitor and being eliminated by the party; nonetheless, it is this same implacable logic which makes him understand and accept the inevitability of his own assassination without malice toward those who have been designated to execute the order. He tells Hugo: "In principle, I have no objection to political assassination. All parties do it.'"[59] However, for those rank-and-file members like the intellectual Hugo who, on the one hand, object to his political tactics, considering them unscrupulous and unethical, but who, on the other hand, would, paradoxically, sacrifice the lives of millions in internecine war rather than accept a compromise, Hoederer labels, in typical Sartrean fashion, cowards. He addresses Hugo, his would-be assassin:

> "How you cling to your purity, young man! How afraid you are to soil your hands! All right, stay pure! What good will it do? Why did you join us? Purity is an idea for a yogi or a monk. You intellectuals and bourgeois anarchists use it as a pretext for doing nothing. To do nothing, to remain motionless, arms at your sides, wearing kid gloves. Well, I have dirty hands. Right up to the elbows. I've plunged them in filth and blood. But what do you hope? Do you think you can govern innocently?"[60]

Reminiscent of Sartre's political views in *Dirty Hands*, Fanon was to write in *The Wretched of the Earth*:

The collective struggle presupposes collective responsibility at the base and collegiate responsibility at the top. Yes, everybody will have to be compromised in the fight for the common good. No one has clean hands; there are no innocents and no onlookers. We all have dirty hands; we are all soiling them in the swamps of our country and in the terrifying emptiness of our brains. Every onlooker is either a coward or a traitor.[61]

Hence, the Marxist precepts of Frantz Fanon, Jean-Paul Sartre, and Ayi Kwei Armah serve not only to corroborate the political parallels between them but serve likewise to mark, respectively, at least at this juncture, their seemingly irreconcilable political differences with Camus.

1. Germaine Brée, *Camus and Sartre: Crisis and Commitment* (New York: Dell Publishers, 1972), 241.

2. Annie Cohen-Solal, *Sartre: A Life*, trans. Anna Cancogni (New York: Pantheon, 1987), 431.

3. Axel Madsen, *Hearts and Minds: The Common Journey of Simone de Beauvoir and Jean-Paul Sartre* (New York: William Morrow and Company, 1977), 226.

4. Gareth Griffiths, "Structure and Image in Kwei Armah's *The Beautyful Ones Are Not Yet Born*," *Studies in Black Literature* 2, no. 2 (summer 1971): 6.

5. Frantz Fanon, *The Wretched of the Earth*, trans. Constance Farrington (New York: Grove Press, 1963), 222.

6. William A. Walker, Jr., "Major Ghanaian Fiction in English: A Study of the Novels of Ayi Kwei Armah and Kofi Awoonor" (Ph.D. diss., University of Texas at Austin, 1975), 201.

7. Ayi Kwei Armah, "African Socialism: Utopian or Scientific?," *Présence Africaine* 64 (1967): 29.

8. Richard Priebe, "The Development of a Mythic Consciousness in West African Literature" (Ph.D. diss., University of Texas at Austin, 1973), 78.

9. Frantz Fanon, *Black Skin, White Masks*, trans. Charles Markmann (New York: Grove Press, 1967), 59-60.

10. Ibid., 63.

11. Jan Carew, "African Literature--From the Breath of Gods," review of *Why Are We So Blest?*, by Ayi Kwei Armah, *The New York Times Book Review*, 14 March 1972, 14.

12. Ayi Kwei Armah, *Why Are We So Blest?* (New York: Anchor Press, 1973), 78. All subsequent references to this edition will appear in the text.

13. Simon Gikandi, *Reading the African Novel* (London: Heinemann, 1987), 95.

14. Norman Albritton Spencer, "Political Consciousness in Modern African Literature: A Study of the Novels of Ayi Kwei Armah" (Ph.D. diss., State University of New York at Stony Brook, 1985), 234.

15. Ayi Kwei Armah, "A Mystification: African Independence Revalued," *Pan-African Journal* 2, no. 2 (spring 1969): 149.

16. O.S. Ogede, "Ayi Kwei Armah in America: The Question of Identity in *Why Are We So Blest?*," *Ariel* 20, no. 4 (October 1990): 63.

17. Robert Fraser, *The Novels of Ayi Kwei Armah* (London: Heinemann, 1980), 50.

18. Robert Fraser, "The American Background in *Why Are We So Blest?*," *African Literature Today* 9 (1978): 42.

19. Ibid., 43.

20. Walker, 162.

21. Spencer, 195.

22. Jean-Paul Sartre, *Being and Nothingness: An Essay in Phenomenological Ontology*, intro. and trans. Hazel Barnes (New York: Philosophical Library, 1956), 371.

23. Ibid., 376.

24. Ibid., 377.

25. Simone de Beauvoir, *The Mandarins*, trans. Leonard M. Friedman (New York: W.W. Norton, 1991), 130.

26. Gikandi, *Reading the African Novel*, 92.

27. K. Damodar Rao, *The Novels of Ayi Kwei Armah* (New Delhi: Prestige, 1993), 85.

28. Edward Lobb, "Personal and Political Fate in Armah's *Why Are We So Blest?*," *World Literature Written in English* 19, no. 1 (1980): 16.

29. Sartre, *Being and Nothingness*, 376.

30. Ibid., 377.

31. Jean-Paul Sartre, *No Exit*, in *No Exit and Three Other Plays* (New York: Knopf, 1955), 46.

32. Fanon, *The Wretched of the Earth*, 94.

33. Ben Obumselu, "Marx, Politics and the African Novel," *Twentieth Century Studies* 10 (December 1973): 112.

34. Ibid., 113.

35. Ibid., 109.

36. Ibid., 111.

37. Ayi Kwei Armah, *Two Thousand Seasons* (London: Heinemann, 1979), 39.

38. Ibid., 16.

39. Ibid., 15.

40. Ibid., 169-70.

41. Ibid., 173.

42. Ibid., 173.

43. Ibid., 197.

44. Kofi Anyidoho, "Historical Realism and the Visionary Ideal: Ayi Kwei Armah's *Two Thousand Seasons," Ufahamu* 11, no. 2 (1981-82): 121.

45. Fanon, *The Wretched of the Earth,* 94.

46. Armah, *Two Thousand Seasons,* 205-6.

47. Jean-Paul Sartre, Preface to *The Wretched of the Earth,* by Frantz Fanon, trans. Constance Farrington (New York: Grove Press, 1963), 25.

48. Albert Camus, "Neither Victims nor Executioners," trans. Dwight Macdonald, *Politics* 4, no. 4 (July-August 1947): 144.

49. Albert Camus, *The Rebel,* trans. Anthony Bower (New York: Knopf, 1956), 251.

50. Ibid., 172-73.

51. Albert Camus, "Preface to Algerian Reports," in his *Resistance, Rebellion, and Death,* trans. Justin O'Brien (New York: Knopf, 1960), 115.

52. Buchi Emecheta, *Destination Biafra* (London: Heinemann, 1982).

53. Fanon, *The Wretched of the Earth,* 83-84.

54. Solal, 333-34.

55. John Cruickshank, *Albert Camus and the Literature of Revolt* (New York: Galaxy Press, 1969), 120.

56. Armah, "African Socialism: Utopian or Scientific?," 15, 8 and 11.

57. Alfred Stern, *Sartre: His Philosophy and Existential Psychoanalysis,* 2nd ed., rev. and enl. (New York: Delacorte Press, 1967), 253.

58. Jean-Paul Sartre, *Critique de la Raison dialectique [Critique of Dialectical Reason]* (Paris: Gallimard Press, 1960), quoted in Alfred Stern, *Sartre: His Philosophy and Existential Psychoanalysis,* 2nd ed., rev. and enl. (New York: Delacorte Press, 1967), 256.

59. Jean-Paul Sartre, *Dirty Hands,* in his *No Exit and Three Other Plays* (New York: Knopf, 1948), 191.

60. Ibid., 223-24.

61. Fanon, *The Wretched of the Earth,* 199.

Chapter 6

Armah's Emergent Pacifism

If our study of Ayi Kwei Armah ended with a discussion of his fourth novel, *Two Thousand Seasons*, it would doubtless reflect a stronger comparison between Sartre and Armah than between Armah and Camus on the basis of their shared views with Frantz Fanon on revolutionary violence; but it would fail, ultimately, to acknowledge Armah's growing disaffection with revolutionary rhetoric and his drift toward pacifist views which, in retrospect, were foreshadowed as early as 1968 with the publication of his first novel, *The Beautyful Ones Are Not Yet Born.*

In the first three novels by Armah a noticeable conflict within the major characters has been the one between activism and quietism. Teacher in *The Beautyful Ones* is described as willfully separated from his acquisitive "loved ones" although the price for his lifestyle of freedom is overwhelming loneliness which he cannot in good faith recommend to the man. Also, the fact that Teacher is described as a frustrated writer places his dilemma in a new symbolic framework, since it reveals the writer as relegated to silence by the material concerns of a decadent society although his desire to be heard is no less strong. This is the implicit meaning of the myth of Plato's cave, which the man remembers and associates with Teacher. That is, Teacher would elect himself as a spokesman and protector of the traditional values which Armah describes as all but lost in contemporary Ghanaian society, but in an absurd universe which rewards corruption and penalizes virtue, Teacher is forever doomed to silence. The thwarted desires of the would-be writer are also the meaning of Teacher's off-hand remark to the man wherein he describes poets as "bandleaders who have failed."[1] Although the man is envious of Teacher because he has escaped "the call of the loved ones," ironically, Teacher's remorse stems precisely from the realization that his own lifestyle reflects a compromise between engagement and quietism. Teacher's confession to the man therefore not only exposes his freedom as impotence, but also reveals his grudging respect for his friend, the man, who is at least *dans le coup:*

> "How can I think I am doing the right thing when I am alone and there are so many I have run from? Who is right at all? I know I have chosen something, but it is not something I would have chosen if I had the power to choose truly. I am just there, and if you think I am happier than you driving out there, you don't know what I feel inside."[2]

The conflict between the social conscience of the intellectual and active engagement is also contained in Armah's second novel, *Fragments.* Baako's former schoolmaster, Ocran, describes Baako's agonizing conflict over artistic relevance as "the ghost of a missionary inside you bullying the artist,"[3] while Baako's grandmother, Naana, refers to his benevolent social zeal as "priest-like."[4] Baako, wanting to do something "useful," had decided, against the best interests of his family, to become a writer, initially turning out didactic scripts at Ghanavision for the cultural enlightenment of the people. What he had not prepared himself for though before his return to Ghana had been the cultural complacency of contemporary Ghana which placed little worth on artistic talent, preferring instead the superficial homilies aimed entirely at securing European endowments. The event described as the Writers' Guild in the chapter entitled "Osagyefo" is a case in point.

Akosua Russell, editor of the literary quarterly, *Kyerema,* conveniently arranges soirées in order to court prospective European benefactors with "a very strong and very healthy interest in the development of robust, indigenous art forms."[5] The programme of events, however, has been for eight years so unswervingly pat as to have become farcical. Lawrence Boateng, editor of *Jungle* magazine and writer in his own right, is invited without fail by Russell to read from his yet unpublished novel while she herself recites her well-worn epic poem, "The Coming of the Brilliant Light of the New Age to Amosema Junction Village." The motivation for this charade is, of course, material interest. The foundation funds collected from the soirées, rather than being properly channeled to cultivate young artistic talent as was intended by the donors, are instead pocketed by Russell as personal income. Boateng's drunken charges of embezzlement during the reading therefore come as a shock to no one; they merely shore up publicly the fraudulence and greed all have recognized but, in their own complacency, have refused to counter.[6]

This same cultural complacency and corruption are likewise seen at Ghanavision, where the Director assigns *all* of the television tapes to cover diplomatic functions rather than allocate a portion of those tapes for creative programming and where the officials, similar to Akosua

Russell, engage unabashedly in corporate theft. Hence the overall effect of this corruption, which subverts Baako's creative aims, is insanity and madness.

Finally, the conflict between the social conscience of the intellectual and active engagement is also contained in Solo Nkonam of *Why Are We So Blest?*. Like Teacher and Baako of *The Beautyful Ones* and *Fragments*, respectively, Solo is described as cursed with a seer's vision which is wontedly sabotaged by the material and nationalistic concerns currently in vogue and, concomitantly, by his manifest worry at seeming to appear different, or un-African. He therefore never writes the two novels of which he feels he is capable: a fanciful novel about the "love" of an African male for a Portuguese female and a psychological novel culled from the collective journals of Modin and Aimée on the sado-masochistic tendencies manifested in the African male enamoured with the white female. Instead he perceives his artistic yearnings as vain, frivolous indulgences.[7] Indeed, the characters depicted in Ayi Kwei Armah's fiction are reminiscent of those found in Simone de Beauvoir's *The Mandarins*, namely, Henri Perron and Robert Dubreuilh who have become split personalities by dint of their alliance, as well as opposition, to the Communist Party. In the words of Dubreuilh: "The part we're trying to play is that of an opposition minority, outside of the Party, but allied with it."[8]

The autobiographical nature of Armah's fiction is clearly evident. In the article "One Writer's Education," the author speaks candidly of the nervous collapse that he suffered approximately nine months after he left Harvard. The collapse was precipitated, in part, by his desire to effectuate change, despite his awareness of the ineffectuality of words:

> How to work up some semblance of motivation for living in a world dying for change, but which I couldn't help to change. I knew I could write, but the question that immobilised me then remains to this day: of what creative use are skilfully arranged words when the really creative work–changing Africa's social realities for the better–remains inaccessible?
>
> When I returned to Ghana in 1964, there was nothing at home so unexpected as to shock me. Rather, I was in the position of a spore which, having finally accepted its destiny as a fungus, still wonders if it might produce penicillin.[9]

One cannot help feeling that the critical views expressed by Chinua Achebe in his article "The Novelist as Teacher" that the African writer should be engagé and that he should select it as his task to re-educate the African people--"to help [the] society regain belief in itself and put away the complexes of the years of denigration and self-abasement"[10]--have had an impact on Armah, perhaps inspiring the conflict so often recognized in his characters and contributing even, alongside Frantz Fanon, to his later pronouncements of commitment in the form of revolutionary violence in both *Why Are We So Blest?* and *Two Thousand Seasons;* however, with the publication of Armah's fifth novel, *The Healers,* Armah seems to be on the verge of abandoning the revolutionary views expressed in *Why Are We So Blest?* and *Two Thousand Seasons* in favor of pacifism.

Even in Armah's first novel, *The Beautyful Ones,* the disillusionment with revolutionary promises was seen as paramount. The characters the man and Teacher spoke of social betrayal, political corruption, and gross defilement of the national consciousness, all of which were centuries-old and which made the moral and spiritual crisis of contemporary Ghana appear the realization of prophecy, since the individuals by and large exerted so little free will and backbone that their political and social roles appeared almost pre-determined. For example, Armah described the corrupt politician Koomson, linking him, subsequently, to the mercenary chiefs of a by-gone era:

> The man, when he shook hands, was again amazed at the flabby softness of the hand. Ideological hands, the hands of revolutionaries leading their people into bold sacrifices, should these hands not have become even tougher than they were when their owner was hauling loads along the wharf? And yet these were the socialists of Africa, fat, perfumed, soft with the ancestral softness of chiefs who have sold their people and are celestially happy with the fruits of the trade.[11]

Also, in *Why Are We So Blest,* a novel dated around 1962 and the period of Algeria's liberation from France, Armah speaks of the hope and promise of the revolutionary movement betrayed by the displacement of national energies towards the courtship of European interests. Hence Armah describes Jorge Manuel's total pre-occupation with foreign journalists and the subsequent neglect of the country's domestic ills. This pre-occupation is seen in Manuel's brusque treatment of the inter-racial couple, Modin and Aimée, when they first arrive at the office of the UPC. One of the reasons Aimée and Modin are not given the time of day is precisely because they lack journalistic credentials. Upon arrival at the office of the UPC, Esteban Ngulo, the assistant to Jorge Manuel, inquires if they are journalists.[12] Additionally, when Modin and Aimée make their way from New York to Washington and finally to Laccryville on their own initiative, they are befriended by three managerial cadres of an occupied French feudal estate who "asked [them] questions, asked what [they] thought of the farm, and generally treated [them] as though [they] were some important foreign journalists." [13]

Even in Armah's most revolutionary novel, *Two Thousand Seasons,*[14] which exhorts the African peoples, moreso than *Why Are We So Blest?,* to root out and destroy all forces contrary to African unity, Armah has been careful to differentiate between a selfish, malevolent, vengeful, and ultimately destructive violence and a violence which fosters wholeness and a return to national unity and health. Hence the call to arms as contained in the novel, rather than becoming a rationale for selfish and perverse motives, becomes instead identifiable with group solidarity and the protection of national interests.

Armah's growing affinity to pacifism, however, is demonstrated more in his fifth novel *The Healers*. In a group of fundis who are aligned with creativity, inspiration, and spirituality, Armah strongly criticizes aggression of any kind, particularly aggression for political ends. In fact, his views grow largely out of his reaction to a group termed the manipulators, largely royals, whose aggression against both the Asante people and against peoples or subjects from other neighboring territories creates internal dissension and strife, thereby paving the way for European intervention and domination.

The thematic purpose of the novel is largely represented in the treatment of the military leader Asamoa Nkwanta, chief commander of the army of Asante, "the soul of the army," who has vowed, after the wanton murder of his favorite nephew, never to touch arms again in defence of Asante.[15]

From conversations with his mentor, Damfo the healer, Densu learns of the circumstances surrounding the murder of Nkwanta's nephew. According to Damfo, it was the custom, following the death of the king, to provide the departed king with slaves in order to ease the king's final journey into death. Royal youths were therefore permitted to raid the countryside in search of victims to send after the dead king. One royal youth Boache Aso, however, had ignored the common practice of killing only the powerless, people without relatives to avenge them, and had taken advantage of the murderous excitement by hunting down and murdering his rival, the commander's favorite nephew, in order to settle a personal score. Nkwanta, threatening first to destroy the murderer of his nephew, was thwarted by the sudden disappearance of the young royal. He then threatened civil war against the royals but was pacified by the royals' consent to sacrifice Opanin Kwamen, an uncle of the prince; however, this peace-making effort by the royals, rather than allaying Nkwanta's sorrow, had only served to deepen it, since Nkwanta recognized in this wanton aggression against innocent victims as mandated by the royals a flagrant violation of human rights which was at the very foundation of the political structure (99).

Because the personal tragedy had forced Nkwanta to evaluate his life and the values of the royals whom he serves and protects, Damfo finds in the reparation of Nkwanta's wounded psyche hopes for the highest form of healing.

112   Existential Fiction

Earlier, Damfo had spoken of the art of healing as a receptivity to the signs of the universe. That is, unlike ordinary men who observe only a surface reality, Damfo had described the healer as possessing a spirit in full communion with nature. He had given the illustration of a child who had been bitten by a snake. A person with "ordinary eyes" would have been able to see only a helpless child lying near death amongst the leaves of the forest; but the healer, in full communion with nature, would have been able to perceive in the foliage the existence of possible antidotes (79).

In addition to "seeing truly, hearing truly, understanding truly, and acting truly" (81), the healers are also described as spiritual medicinemen whose aim is to achieve the unification of body and spirit; of tribes, nations, and people, the latter becoming in the context of the novel identified with nationalism. Damfo had equated the first order of healing to "inspiration"--the devout respect for the integrity of the individual and the refusal to reduce individuals to human pawns through deceit. An example of the first order of healing is found in Araba Jesiwa, daughter of the queen mother at Esuano and mother of the murdered prince, Appia.

Described as a woman frustrated by her barrenness, Araba had received from Damfo the encouragement for her own liberation. Deceived into thinking that the right thing to do was to marry a royal because she was a royal, Araba had done violence to her soul by marrying a man whom she did not love: Bedu Addo, one of the royals. The result of this unhappy union was, seemingly, barrenness. At least four times Araba had conceived, and the same number of times she had aborted. The failure to carry a baby to term had led her to seek out a number of herbalists whose concoctions from snakes, rhinos, lizards, spiders, and scorpions were supposed to make her fertile; however, only after Araba Jesiwa's contact with the healer Damfo was she able to recognize that the abortions had been acts of will and that only after her divorce from Addo and her union with the craftsman Entsua, her true soul mate, would the constraints upon her ability to reproduce be removed. Predictably, almost a year following Araba's break with Bedu Addo and her subsequent marriage to Entsua, the two had brought forth the child, Appia. As Araba explains now to Densu, her indebtedness to Damfo the healer is therefore the result of a personal form of healing engendered through greater awareness, honesty, and a truthfulness to one's self (78).

Robert Fraser finds represented in Araba Jesiwa a betrayal of herself which is symptomatic of the nation's betrayal, through competitive, self-serving interests, of the communal spirit of the Akan people. In *The Novels of Ayi Kwei Armah*, he writes:

The betrayal of Araba Jesiwa of her true interests in favour of a borrowed ideal is but a picture in miniature of the situation in which the whole of Asante society finds itself. The original ideal of Akan 'wholeness' has been ditched in a surfeit of social competitiveness and a notion of purely individual advancement. The inevitable concomitants of this process—slavery, the rise of an oligarchic ruling class, fragmentation into jostling ethnic sub-groups—act as a blight on the whole texture of the community's life. It is part of the healers' ultimate purpose to wean society away from enslavement to these false idols, to which it is seemingly as addicted as were the emergent bourgeoisie of Armah's earlier books to the bright gleam emanating from the cocktail cabinet and the chrome panelling.[16]

Examples of the competitiveness of spirit which Armah considers responsible for the fall of the Asante empire are contained throughout the novel, notably in the chapter "Whirlpool," which describes the annual games of initiation.

It is learned that the people of Esuano annually commemorated a common heritage by allowing the generation of youths crossing into manhood to engage in competitive games of strength and skill and endurance. The games now though are described by Armah as a perversion of memory because, contrary to the earlier games which celebrated a communal spirit, the current games, in their degree of competitiveness, have served merely to become divisive (6).

Exemplary of the feelings of rivalry and jealousy engendered by the games are those revealed by Buntui and Anan and by Kojo Djan and Appia respectively. Both Buntui and Kojo Djan, in their thoroughgoing attempts to best their opponents, disregard totally the rules of gamesmanship, which are to put the opponent down in three clean falls, not to maim the opponent, and to release the opponent immediately after he has made the sign of defeat—an arm raised, the index finger extended skyward (10). Buntui ignores Anan's sign of concession and presses his advantage by resorting to headlocks, while the stubborn Kojo Djan even fails to concede defeat, thus forcing the match to be declared a draw, since the young prince Appia cannot accept the price of a forced victory. Earlier, Densu, from an aversion to the sport of wrestling, had given the sign of defeat rather than participate in the matches.

Another example of the destructively competitive nature of Asante society as described by Armah is the politically-motivated murder of the young prince Appia, almost immediately following his declared victory in the games of youth (51). It is learned that the manipulator Ababio, henchman and a member of the royal court, had ruthlessly plotted the murder of the young prince in order to remove roadblocks from the path of European intervention in Esuano and to smooth the way for his own possible succession to the throne by default. Citing the king's age and the influence on Appia of his mother, Araba Jesiwa, who "worships that mad healer, that homeless, wifeless wretch who lives in the eastern forest" (30-31), Ababio, the guardian of Densu, had tempted Densu with the offer of succession if he would comply with European interests, thereby placing himself on the side of opportunity (29). Densu alienates himself, though, from Ababio by refusing to have anything to do with the plot, himself being drawn spiritually to the healers of the eastern forest. Ababio feels, however, that his self-disclosure to Densu has already made him an accessory (47).

The most cogent example, however, of the ruinously competitive nature of the Ashantis is represented, as mentioned above, in the historical treatment of the military leader Asamoa Nkwanta. Described as debilitated by angst related to the spurious use of his life's work fighting internecine wars (183), the only redeeming value he is therefore able to recognize is in possible conflict with the British because of the ideal it would represent to teach his men military strategy (181). According to Nkwanta, war with the British would be essentially a tactical war, not necessarily one based on military might and arms superiority. Aware that the whites are not on friendly terms with the surrounding universe (182), Nkwanta had devised a plan which would defeat the British with the aid of the natural environment. Recalling the fishermen's technique of entrapment, Nkwanta would lead the British army into the forest, entrap them there, and prolong the fighting in order to exact heavy casualties.

In lieu of the above, when the members of the royal court invite Nkwanta, coincident with his recovery, to resume his leadership of the army, Nkwanta heeds the call of the warrior still within him. The circumstances themselves are ripe for his return. The reader learns that the Asante army, an immobilized lot, is threatening the security of the country. The European threat has become a real one with Captain Glover and General Wolseley busily marshaling troops on the coast in order to counter and stultify the Asante aggression against their coastal neighbors. In the chapter "Cape Coast" of Part Six, after Densu is sent by Nkwanta to the coast to gather an intelligence report on the Europeans, he learns of the conditions of European protection. Military weapons, advisors, and food will be supplied by the British, in return for the provision of manpower from the protected territories. And as an added incentive, ten English pounds will be given each month to the king who supplies a thousand warriors. The stakes themselves in this British-Ashanti confrontation are high. According to Basil Davidson who discusses in *The African Slave Trade* the intervention of the British in Asante, at stake here is an unchallenged monopoly of the coast. According to Davidson, the Ashanti Union, recognized in the hinterland during the nineteenth century as a powerful military force, had adopted an expansionist policy which would fortify its control in the hinterland but which would establish it as well as a major power on the coast.[17] This bold bid for sovereignty, however, was to bring Ashanti into inevitable conflict with the Europeans who, in many instances, had been called upon by the coastal states to intervene on their behalf against Ashanti aggression and who themselves, in Davidson's view, "were ceasing to be content with a partnership in Africa in which they were the lesser power."[18]

The outcome of the Ashanti-British conflict is therefore, predictably, invasion and occupation of Kumase, "the virgin capital, Kumase the impregnable stronghold, Kumase the evergreen garden" (243), an outcome which, importantly, Armah attributes to the divisiveness caused by suspicion, jealousy, and rivalry incited by the royals. For example, when Nkwanta presents to the members of the royal council his strategy for defense against the British, following his resumption as commander of the army, they peremptorily accept his defense plan, only to reject it later in a closed session presided over by the queen mother. The queen mother had called for the rejection of Nkwanta's proposal on the grounds that it was contrary to the council's best interests. In other words, the queen mother had classified Nkwanta as an interloper and had argued convincingly that if Nkwanta claimed responsibility for the successful defense of Kumase, nothing would prevent him from seizing power and claiming the kingship for himself. She therefore had counseled surrender to the British (291).

The upshot is that Nkwanta, unaware of the betrayal, is forced to make a stand below Amoafo, fighting with only the front "net" of the army, the remainder of the army which was to serve as the enclosing net and which was to block the enemy's escape having deserted or withdrawn under orders from the king. Importantly, though, the possibility of betrayal had been foreseen by Nkwanta in his disclosure to Damfo. That is, despite the virtual infallibility of the plan, Nkwanta had predicted its failure based upon the royals' chronic fear of usurpation (182-83).

Thematically, in view of the above, it may be argued that *The Healers* follows roughly the pattern of Chinua Achebe's *Things Fall Apart*. Similar to Achebe, Armah probes into the past of African societies, notably the Asante kingdom, in order to analyze the reasons for its subjugation to the British, ultimately concluding that the reason for the fall of the Asante kingdom was the fragmentation created largely by inter-tribal wars, the practice by the royals of elitist or exclusionary politics, and the subsequent inability of the Akan people to mobilize themselves to fend off an outside attack. Also, similar to Achebe, Armah calls to task certain blind religious practices which likewise reveal a diseased body politic.

On one occasion, the Asantehene had called upon the priests to interpret the ominous sign of the fallen odum tree in the capital of Kumase, which had symbolized "the mighty Asante family with its wide spreading branches" (250). The priests, not wanting to be the direct bearer of the terrible news, had chosen indirection. They had ordered two slaves selected for sacrificial deaths (251). Two slaves were found, their tongues were skewered, and they were tied fast to two trees in the Swamp of the Dead and left there to die a natural death, the priests having told the Asantehene that the fate of the nation would depend on the nature of their deaths. Taken as an evil portent is the fact that the two slaves did not die until the sixth and ninth days respectively.

On another occasion, with the news of the advancing European army led by General Wolseley, the Asantehene had once again consulted with the priests and had been advised on the necessity of choosing, in this particular instance, only the fittest of human subjects for sacrifice, subjects whose bodies were duly mutilated in order to frighten the advancing army away from Kumase (282).

Earlier, Armah had described the rudderless Asante army, without their commander, Nkwanta, attempting to cross the perilous river Pra to re-possess dissident Assin districts forfeited by the Anglo-Asante treaty of 1831 to European jurisdiction[19] and making human sacrifices to the river Pra in efforts to make more propitious their crossing.

This thematic development follows largely the pattern of Chinua Achebe's novel *Things Fall Apart*, published in 1959, wherein the novelist cites as one contributory cause of the fall of the Ibo clan the ostracism of misfits like the *efulefu*, "worthless, empty men,"[20] and outcasts like the *osu*, "a person dedicated to a god, a thing set apart,"[21] who, consequently, found refuge in European Christianity.

The historian Ivor Wilks, however, finds in the Asantehene's reversion to fetishism a principal lack of faith in the usual diplomatic channels, the mark of whose failure was the Europeans' adamant refusal to respond in like fashion to the Asantehene's entreaties of peace. In his work *Asante in the Nineteenth Century*, he concludes:

> As its [the government's] requests to Wolseley to halt the offensive operations and negotiate a settlement were one after the other rejected, so the government came to realize that it had totally lost political initiative to the British. The indications are, that in the circumstances of acute crisis the Asantehene Kofi Kakari turned for advice away from both councillors and counselors, and increasingly to the religious authorities--including those natural allies in his struggle against the Europeans, the powerful Muslim notables of the northern hinterlands.[22]

Ayi Kwei Armah, on the other hand, finds implicit in this wanton violation of human life a perpetuation of the caste system which has slavery and servitude at its base, since the royals are insulated by birthright against the persecution which they so arbitrarily inflict upon their subjects. In a rare moment of insight, the mother to the Asantehene had acknowledged that the signs of impending doom were evidence of a spiritual malignancy (279). On the metaphoric use by Ayi Kwei Armah of disease in *The Healers,* Derek Wright has made the following critical observation:

> Disease, as a metaphor of disintegration, becomes a symbolic catch-all accommodating many different kinds of personal and collective disunity, all of which are seen confusingly in terms of one another: the image ranges over the physical disease that rots the army, the psychosomatic complications of Araba's traumatic illness, the spiritual suffering of Asamoa and the deeper moral sickness of Ababio and the court intriguers. . . . The result is that the concept threatens to become an intellectual vacuum into which almost anything can be put.[23]

Thus it is largely out of reaction to the ruthless and inhumane politics as practiced by the royals, or the manipulators, which leads Ayi Kwei Armah to adopt the relative views of pacifism. When Densu had come under Damfo's tutelage to learn the art of healing, he had been instructed on the seven rules or commandments which would-be healers must abide by and accept in order to ensure the vocation of healing as their proper calling. Importantly, two of those commandments were to abstain from both politics and violence. On the latter, Damfo had remarked to Densu that the apprentice healer does not fight (92).

It is also the healer Damfo's faith in inspiration or pacifism, as it were, which leads Damfo to withdraw from the war front following the recovery of Nkwanta rather than risk compromising these commandments. Acknowledging that in coming to Praso he had hoped to move towards the greater healing work (269), Damfo refuses to exact that triumph by turning Nkwanta into an instrument for the albeit worthy nationalistic aims of the healers. Also, notwithstanding the good intentions of Nkwanta in wanting to further the cause of African unity, Damfo recognizes that Nkwanta is caught up in the contradiction of aspiring to do good while in the service of those who thrive on dissension. Finally, Damfo defends his withdrawal from Praso by noting to the other healers that "this is seed time" (270), and that the time is not yet ripe for the radical change that would effect a classless society, thus eliminating the schisms among the Akan people which, according to Armah, are the enemies of nationalism.

It must be noted, though, that despite Armah's criticism of the Ashanti Union, the conclusion of the novel itself is optimistic. In the final chapter, "The New Dance," Armah describes the victorious departure of General Wolseley from the coast by sea, to the accompaniment of music being played by the West Indian soldiers, and the atmosphere of festive merrymaking, following his departure, which, for a time, imparted a fleeting sensation of brotherhood amongst the myriad groups of African men from Dahomey, Anecho, Atakpame, Ada, Ga, and Ekuapem gathered there (309).

Neil Lazarus, in his article "Techniques in Armah's *The Healers,* argues that the model for Armah's work may have been the historical epic *Chaka* by the Sotho author Mokopu Mofolo on which Armah had written in a journal article. Similar to Chaka, Densu's growth is related to a series of crises:

> Just as, according to Armah, Mofolo stages Chaka's growth as a series of crises, the supercession of each of which results in the individual Chaka's being somewhat changed or altered, newly situated, having a different horizon and a longer, more mediated history, so too Armah presents Densu's growth to maturity as a cumulative sequence of key moments.[24]

Finally, Charles Larson in his review of Armah's fourth novel, *Two Thousand Seasons,* had described the departure of the work from Armah's previous works as indicative of Armah's "continuous growth as a writer; his ability to strike into new areas and not to write the same novel over and over again as so many writers (not just African writers) do throughout their careers."[25] This assessment may also be applied to Armah's fifth novel, *The Healers,* since likewise it reveals the writer able to stretch and to modify his earlier views in order to accommodate his growth as a writer. Throughout the literature by Armah, however, there has been, consistently, the reluctance to endorse any views wholesale or unreservedly; hence the reader finds a divided consciousness like Solo's in *Why Are We So Blest?* and Teacher's in *The Beautyful Ones Are Not Yet Born* which accepts, theoretically, the logic of revolutionary commitment but which, at the same time, retains tenaciously the right to dissent on the grounds of the characters' own ability to choose. The failure to assume an absolutist perspective toward the world has likewise been the mark of both Camus and Sartre, most notably of Camus who, following *The Myth of Sisyphus,* altered the nihilistic views of the absurd as contained therein to the more hopeful ones of revolt as outlined in *The Rebel.*

To recapitulate, in *The Myth of Sisyphus,* Camus had argued, as had Sartre, the relativity of all human values. That is, Camus had argued that if the world is absurd and if God does not exist, there is no pre-established moral ethic to which man can defer. Man is beholden to no one and therefore can regulate his values only as he sees fit. He can neither be criticized nor condoned since, in an absurd universe, there is no *a priori* of values against which he can either be measured or censured. According to John Cruickshank, however, in his work *Albert Camus and the Literature of Revolt,* Camus's active participation in the

French Resistance led to a re-examination of the conclusions arrived at in *The Myth of Sisyphus*. This *examen de conscience* which had begun during the period of the French Resistance has been, subsequently, set forth in Camus's *Lettres à un ami allemand*, letters which were published clandestinely during the Occupation.

In a series of four letters, Camus had eschewed his former absurdist position as too anarchist and nihilistic. That is, starting from the same philosophical position of the absurd, Camus and his German friend had arrived at two opposite sets of conclusions. The German friend averred that "in a world where everything has lost its meaning, those who, like us young Germans, are lucky enough to find a meaning in the destiny of our nation must sacrifice everything else."[26] Here was an attitude of complete abandon which Camus, despite having defended it in *The Myth of Sisyphus*, could not accept. According to John Cruickshank, the particular or concrete situation of the French Resistance proved the quantitative ethic of the absurdist philosophy to be unacceptable. He continues: "Moral choices and responsibilities arose which could mean life or death for others, depending on how they were interpreted. An instinctive moralist like Camus was unable to put the quisling or the informer on a level with the Resistance fighter."[27] The philosophy Camus was to articulate in *The Rebel* became therefore Camus's own reasoned justification for the reactionary views expressed in *Lettres à un ami allemand*. The work represents Camus's attempt to find some middle ground between the nihilism of *The Myth of Sisyphus*, which eschewed moral absolutes, and the religious optimism recognized in the philosophers of despair, Chestov, Kierkegaard, and Jaspers. This middle ground Camus found in the philosophy of revolt, which did not betray the tension between negation and affirmation to the extremities of nihilism, violence, and/or murder. As Camus was to argue in the fourth letter, the difference between him and his German friend was that the German friend had given in to despair while he had never yielded to it:

I continue to believe that this world has no ultimate meaning. But I know that something in it has a meaning and that is man, because he is the only creature to insist on having one. This world has at least the truth of man, and our task is to provide its justification against fate itself. And it has no justification but man; hence he must be saved if we want to save the idea we have of life. . . . And with all my being I shout to you that I mean not mutilating him and yet giving a chance to the justice that man alone can conceive.[28]

Implicit in Camus's views as expressed in his *Lettres à un ami allemand* is the reason for his disavowal of himself as an existentialist. Unlike Sartre who had denied the existence of God and, concomitantly, the existence of any universal value, Camus recognized a solidarity of experience which he had referred to in his letters as the concept of mankind which he deemed worthy of support and defense; nonetheless, despite the discrepant views between Camus and Sartre on the major tenet of the philosophy, it may be argued that Camus remains an existentialist by virtue of his humanistic perspective which parallels that of both Jean-Paul Sartre and Ayi Kwei Armah.

In the essay *Existentialism and Humanism*, Sartre had noted in the opening statement that the purpose of the work was "to offer a defence of existentialism against several reproaches that have been laid against it."[29] Commonly, those reproaches are that the philosophy is too despairing, since it harps on "all that is ignominious in the human situation, . . . mean, sordid or base to the neglect of certain things that possess charm and beauty and belong to the brighter side of human nature,"[30] and that the philosophy, in its complete subjectivism, encourages anarchy, since in a world described as devoid of a moral center, anything goes. Sartre had considered the first charge unfounded, rejoining that "the excessive protests" of those who complain that "existentialism is too gloomy a view of things" make me suspect that "what is annoying them is not so much our pessimism, but, much more likely, our optimism."[31] Sartre had supported that claim by noting the ascendancy given by the philosophy to individual choice. Identifying as the common denominator amongst existentialists the belief that *"existence* comes before *essence*-or, if you will, that we must begin from the subjective,"[32] Sartre found in the denial of a pre-existing moral or ethical center the basis for limitless possibilities in that man is able to invent himself, free of all prior constraints. To be sure, along with this complete free choice comes the anguish of responsibility, since man can no longer attribute to fate or to circumstances the responsibility for his own shortcomings. According to Sartre, "In life, a man commits himself, draws his own portrait and there is nothing but that portrait."[33]

To the reproach that existentialism traps man within his own subjectivity, Sartre had countered that any theory that begins outside the Cartesian *cogito, I think, therefore I am,* which establishes the proof of human existence, falls prey to treating man as an object, or "a set of pre-determined reactions, in no way different from the patterns of qualities and phenomena which constitute a table, or a chair or a stone."[34]

Hence, in light of the above, Sartre had concluded that "what people reproach us with is not, after all, our pessimism, but the sternness of our optimism,"[35] justifying, in the end, the fundamental humanism of a philosophy which has man as its complete center of reference. He has contended:

> There is no other universe except the human universe, the universe of human subjectivity. This relation of transcendence as constitutive of man (not in the sense

that God is transcendent, but in the sense of self-surpassing) with subjectivity (in such a sense that man is not shut up in himself but forever present in a human universe)--it is this that we call existential humanism. This is humanism, because we remind man that there is no legislator but himself; that he himself, thus abandoned, must decide for himself; also because we show that it is not by turning back upon himself, but always by seeking, beyond himself, an aim which is one of liberation or of some particular realisation, that man can realise himself as truly human.[36]

This humanistic approach to philosophy has also been at the root of Sartre's differences with Marxists. Sartre, despite his sympathy with the aims of the working class, refused to join the Communist party because he opposed the sacrifice of individuality to dialectical materialism. Expressive of this sentiment is the character Henri Perron in Simone de Beauvoir's *The Mandarins:* "What he held against them [the Communist Party] most of all was treating people as things; if you didn't believe in their right to freedom, in their good will, then individuals weren't bothering about."[37] Sartre's philosophical work *The Critique de la Raison dialectique* represents therein the writer's own attempt to resolve the differences between the subjectivism of his philosophy and the collectivism of Marxism by imbuing the latter with a human element.

The existentialist perspective of Ayi Kwei Armah is similarly seen in his indefatigable defense of the integrity of the common man whom he describes as often the victim of political and social corruption. This concern by Armah is shown in his description in *The Beautyful Ones* of the man and his family who are reduced to sub-humans by their severe poverty, the mark of which is a crowded bungalow and a filth-, stench-ridden, roach-infested communal latrine. When Koomson visits the home of the man to discuss the arrangements for his illegal boat enterprise, he abstains from using the lavatory facilities, being at once put off by the filth and stench. A description of Koomson's reaction to the facilities is given below.

The boy, in the light filtering through from the open doorway of the latrine, appeared still to be wiping his left hand on a piece of leftover newspaper. As he advanced past the waiting pair, a stench came up behind him like a sea wave and hit the men directly in the face. Koomson let a small gasp escape him, hesitated at the door, then, with just a single glance into the entrails of the latrine, he turned back. He said nothing to the man, and the man did not ask him anything. There was no need for words.[38]

In contrast to the wretched poverty of the man, however, is the grand, showcase lifestyle of Joe Koomson which is symbolically reflected in objects of chrome. When the man and his wife visit the Koomson home to sign the documents which would designate them as ghost owners of Koomson's fishing boat, the man inspects the gleaming objects of chrome which decorate the living room and which have come to symbolize, within the context of the novel, Koomson's fraudulent wealth. He remarks that

> It was amazing how much light there was in a place like this. It glinted off every object in the room. Next to each ashtray there were two shiny things: a silver box and a small toy-like pistol. The man wondered what the pistols were for. Light came off the marble tops of the little side tables. People had wondered what use a State Marble Works Corporation could be. They need not have wondered. There were uses here.[39]

Armah's defense of the common man victimized by greed is also revealed in *Fragments* through the censorious tone of his description of the larceny as practiced by the officials of Ghanavision and by Akosua Russell of the literary quarterly *Kyerema;* in *Why Are We So Blest?* through the juxtaposition of the beleaguered orphans described by Armah as destitute of hope and the flamboyant and decadent lifestyle of the mulatto Jorge Manuel who has benefited from the political upheaval created by Algeria's successful bid for independence; and, finally, in the works *Two Thousand Seasons* and *The Healers* through his depiction, respectively, of the atrocity of the African slave trade and the sell-out of the Asante to the Europeans for the sake of "hot drinks," gold, trinkets, and tinsel. Of the latter, Armah describes in *The Healers* the betrayal of the Asante by the coastal states to the British, in return for large bottles of gin, bright new guns, ammunition, and shiny coins (259). Hence, in lieu of the above, *The Healers,* despite appearing at face value to differ from Armah's previous novels *Why Are We So Blest?* and *Two Thousand Seasons* because of its emergent pacifist views, nonetheless, is linked to the previous novels by virtue of its criticism of crass materialism which jeopardizes the spirit of nationalism, calls into question the existential precepts of freedom, choice, and personal responsibility, and, consequently, reduces men to beasts of prey adept in the vile practice of social and political exploitation.

Complementary to the existentialist view of "the absolute character of free commitment"[40] is likewise Armah's view of alienation as a pre-condition to individual freedom. Consistently, in Armah's first three novels the writer identifies the major characters as uprooted intellectuals who are alienated from family and society. Teacher in *The Beautyful Ones* has willfully severed his ties from family and society, existing now in a primeval state of disconnectedness and innocence which is reflected in his own naked form. Similarly, the man, although he is described as not without "loved ones," is separated from them by dint of his morality which cannot condone the corrupt moneyed values imported from the West. Importantly, he considers Teacher "the freest person I know" because, unlike himself and others, "'You have escaped the call of the loved ones.'"[41] Likewise Baako in *Fragments* is described by Armah as alienated from his family members because of his uncompromising morality which will not allow him to stoop to self-betterment at the cost of prostituting himself as an artist.

The ultimate existential hero, however, is the character Solo Nkonam in Armah's *Why Are We So Blest?* who, like the man in *The Beautyful Ones*, is both spiritually and physically alienated from family and society as a result of his incessant brooding over esoteric concerns. In *Two Thousand Seasons* Armah had openly criticized domestic or familial involvement on the grounds that, as represented in the man's unwitting involvement in Koomson's boat scheme in *The Beautyful Ones*, it often led to an uneasy compromise of moral values. In the chapter entitled "The Voice," Armah had equated the call of "the loved ones" to "a call of death," since the strain of the spirit was often towards the nostalgic past, towards a universe inhabited by like "shrunken souls" complacent in their own destruction. Hence Armah had written unsympathetically of the return of Dovi, a member of the rebel group, to Anoa, regarding it as both selfishness and cowardice.[42]

The alienation of the individual as a pre-condition to human freedom is likewise the measure of the bachelor heroes Meursault in Camus's *The Stranger;* Roquentin, in Sartre's *La Nausée;* Mathieu, in Sartre's *The Age of Reason;* and Hoederer, in Sartre's drama *Dirty Hands,* to name but a few. In Sartre's *The Age of Reason,* Mathieu, the fictional homologue of Sartre, despite the social pressure placed on him to conform, refuses to marry his pregnant mistress, Marcelle, seeing only in the prospect an absolute defeat which would rival that of the married men he had encountered with "four children, unfaithful wives, members of the Parents' Association . . . fleshy, neatly dressed, rather facetious, and with celluloid eyes."[43]

The example *par excellence* of the free individual is, respectively, Jean-Paul Sartre and his life-long mate, Simone de Beauvoir, who jointly rejected the "bourgeois" concept of marriage as an undue compromise of their existentialist principles. According to Maurice Cranston, "Depressed by prolonged separations, they [Sartre and Simone de Beauvoir] seriously contemplated marriage, but finally decided that as they did not intend to have children there was no justification for compromising with their progressive principles; and they never married."[44] Indicative of their life-long companionship, which was meant to represent a relationship in good faith, is the characterization in Simone de Beauvoir's novel *She Came to Stay* of the fictitious counterparts Pierre--a writer, actor, and director--and Francoise--also a writer--who for ten years have sustained a free, reciprocal, and non-binding relationship. That is, for ten years they have traveled and worked together, but have maintained separate residences and have indulged the flirtatious, intermittent affairs of the other out of respect for the other's covetous desire for freedom. In typical existentialist fashion, the heroine proclaims the ideal of a relationship practiced in good faith where both individuals exist as subjects, not giving sway to sado-masochism:

> "Yes. I've never had any difficulty with you, because I barely distinguish you from myself."
> "And besides, between us there's reciprocation."
> "How do you mean?"
> "The moment you acknowledge my conscience, you know that I acknowledge one in you, too. That makes all the difference."
> "Perhaps," said Francoise. She stared in momentary perplexity at the bottom of her glass. "In short, that is friendship. Each renounces his pre-eminence. But what if either one refuses to renounce it?"
> "In that case, friendship is impossible," said Pierre.[45]

In conclusion, the fundamental existentialist concepts which link Ayi Kwei Armah, Jean-Paul Sartre, and Albert Camus are these: their respective belief(s) in the self-containment of the individual due to an absurd and indifferent universe and in the necessity, therefore, of choice and commitment, whether manifested in revolt or revolution; and in their collective humanistic perspective which considers the violation of man's free will in the interest of either political or social efficacy the ultimate human transgression. As Jean-Paul Sartre was to write for *Les Tempes modernes* in honor of Camus's memory:

> [Camus] represented in this century, and against History, the present heir of that long line of moralists whose works perhaps constitute what is most original in French letters. His stubborn humanism, narrow and pure, austere and sensual, waged a dubious battle against events of these times. But inversely, through the obstinacy of his refusals, he reaffirmed the existence of moral fact within the heart of our era and against the Machiavellians, against the golden calf of realism.[46]

Hence, Germaine Brée's critical summary of Albert Camus in her comparative work, *Camus and Sartre: Crisis and Commitment,* may likewise be considered applicable to both Ayi Kwei Armah and Jean-Paul Sartre, since it summarizes, effectively, the humanistic attitudes shared and defended by the writers in their respective body of works:

> His [Camus's] goal was to enhance life, not to destroy it. The same creative urge lay behind his political commitments and his work, however much they might on the surface appear to run counter to each other. He could not be an absolutist. . .

. He would make his mistakes and live his own passions. And he would struggle to realize in himself the goal he hoped might be reached by all men. He "possessed violence" in a time of great violence, and so strove mightily "to acquire measure." By the late thirties Camus had rejected the role of revolution, but not his original premises. There are rights and wrongs in human affairs; the wrongs can be intolerable. He was committed to fight against them, as he encountered them in their immediacy here and now according to his own views and capabilities; and, as far as possible without losing sight of his goal, to develop all his possibilities, not least among them his possibilities as an artist; for in the discipline they required of him was a source of equilibrium for him and a way open to understanding. Throughout the war it helped him maintain his sanity; and throughout the years the balance between his public and his personal life.[47]

1. Ayi Kwei Armah, *The Beautyful Ones Are Not Yet Born* (New York: Houghton Mifflin, 1968), 51.

2. Ibid., 59.

3. Ayi Kwei Armah, *Fragments* (New York: Collier Books, 1969), 120.

4. Ibid., 222.

5. Ibid., 161.

6. Ibid., 168.

7. Ayi Kwei Armah, *Why Are We So Blest?* (New York: Anchor Press, 1973), 232.

8. Simone de Beauvoir, *The Mandarins*, trans. Leonard M. Friedman (New York: W.W. Norton, 1991), 241-42.

9. Ayi Kwei Armah, "One Writer's Education," *West Africa*, 26 August 1985, 1753.

10. Chinua Achebe, "The Novelist as Teacher," in his *Morning Yet on Creation Day* (New York: Anchor/Doubleday Press, 1975), 71.

11. Armah, *The Beautyful Ones*, 129-30.

12. Armah, *Why Are We So Blest?*, 59.

13. Ibid., 242.

14. Ayi Kwei Armah, *Two Thousand Seasons* (London: Heinemann, 1979), 205.

15. Ayi Kwei Armah, *The Healers* (London: Heinemann, 1979), 98. All subsequent references to this edition will appear in the text.

16. Robert Fraser, *The Novels of Ayi Kwei Armah* (London: Heinemann, 1980), 92.

17. Basil Davidson, *The African Slave Trade: Precolonial History 1450-1850* (Boston: Little, Brown, 1961), 254.

18. Ibid., 254.

19. Ivor Wilks, *Asante in the Nineteenth Century: The Structure and Evolution of a Political Order* (London: Cambridge UP, 1975), 190-91.

20. Chinua Achebe, *Things Fall Apart* (London: Heinemann, 1959), 130.

21. Ibid., 143.

22. Wilks, 238-39.

23. Derek Wright, *Ayi Kwei Armah's Africa: The Sources of His Fiction* (London: Hans Zell Publishers, 1989), 253-54.

24. Neil Lazarus, "Technique in Armah's *The Healers,*" *Research in African Literatures* 13, no. 4 (1982): 496.

25. Charles Larson, "Ayi Kwei Armah's Vision of Reciprocity," review of *Two Thousand Seasons,* by Ayi Kwei Armah (London: Heinemann, 1979), *Africa Today* 21, no. 2 (March 1974): 119.

26. Albert Camus, "Letters to a German Friend," in *Resistance, Rebellion, and Death,* trans. Justin O'Brien (New York: Alfred Knopf, 1960), 5.

27. John Cruickshank, *Albert Camus and the Literature of Revolt* (Oxford: Oxford UP, 1960), 92.

28. Camus, "Letters to a German Friend," in *Resistance, Rebellion, and Death,* 28-29.

29. Jean-Paul Sartre, *Existentialism and Humanism,* trans. Philip Mairet (London: Methuen, 1948), 23.

30. Ibid., 23.

31. Ibid., 25.

32. Ibid., 26.

33. Ibid., 42.

34. Ibid., 45.

35. Ibid., 42.

36. Ibid., 55-56.

37. Simone de Beauvoir, *The Mandarins,* 241-42.

38. Armah, *The Beautyful Ones,* 133.

39. Ibid., 144-45.

40. Sartre, *Existentialism and Humanism,* 47.

41. Armah, *The Beautyful Ones,* 54.

128   Existential Fiction

42. Armah, *Two Thousand Seasons*, 199.

43. Jean-Paul Sartre, *The Age of Reason*, trans. Eric Sutton (New York: Alfred Knopf, 1947), 124.

44. Maurice Cranston, *Jean-Paul Sartre* (New York: Grove Press, 1962), 3.

45. Simone de Beauvoir, *She Came to Stay*. (New York: W.W. Norton and Company, 1954), 301-2.

46. Annie Cohen-Solal, *Sartre: A Life*, trans. Anna Cancogni (New York: Pantheon, 1987), 435.

47. Germaine Brée, *Camus and Sartre: Crisis and Commitment* (New York: Dell, 1972), 150.

Chapter 7

Conclusion

The views presented in the novels of Ayi Kwei Armah are by no means unique. The depiction of Europeans as destroyers, the characterization that has earned Armah the label of an "anti-racial racist," can be found in the literature of other West African and West Indian authors whose cultural awakening gave ascent to a nationalist fervor. In fact, Eustace Palmer in "Negritude Re-discovered: A Reading of the Recent Novels of Armah, Ngugi, and Soyinka" identifies, among others, the hostility associated with whites in the literature by Armah as a characteristic that the writers share with the old Negritude school of thought, the distinction being that whereas the old Negritudinists were inward looking, the new Negritudinists are more forward looking: "The new Negritude, . . . while sharing many of the characteristics of the old, is more positive, more confident, less introspective, more aggressive. It derives its inspiration not so much from a contemplation of what Africa was, as from a determination to bring about what it ought to be."[1] One could also add to the list the Nigerian author Buchi Emecheta and the Caribbean author Simone Schwarz-Bart whose respective works reflect a similar racialism.

Conceptualized as myth, Simone Schwarz-Bart in *Between Two Worlds* narrates the events that have plunged Guadeloupe and Fond-Zombi into darkness. A Spirit, referred to as "the Beast," has devoured everything in its path--men, rivers, suns and moons. Ti Jean, the hero of the novel, is also devoured by the Beast; however, endowed with supernatural powers, he destroys the Beast, but not before he journeys to Africa and the Kingdom of the Dead, traversing generations of time, in the innards of the Beast.

The tale of Ti Jean's conquest of the Beast is a mixture of legend, myth, and fable, as revealed by the rendition told by a Wanderer in the

Kingdom of the Dead. Nonetheless, the tales coalesce at the end of the hero's journey as, true to legend, Ti Jean liberates the sun, moon, stars, and creatures imprisoned inside the Beast by slitting the Beast's stomach with a machete. The description of the Beast, emblematic of the evil of white dominance, is telling:

> It resembled a cow, but it was as tall as several ordinary cows, with a human-looking muzzle and two rows of lyre-shaped horns on its head forming a sort of crown. It was lying on its side, its bright white coat sparkling with long, silky, transparent fair hairs.[2]

Similarly, the rapaciousness of Europeans has been identified in Emecheta's *Destination Biafra*. Set on the eve of the newly-independent Nigeria's first democratic election and the pursuant Nigerian civil war of 1967-70,[3] Emecheta outlines the reasons for the internecine war among the various ethnic groups: the Hausas, the Yorubas, and the Ibos. The English Governor Macdonald, contrary to the popular will of the people who favor the Igbo leader Dr. Ozimba, member of the NCNC/UPC, appoints a Hausa, Mallam Nguru Kano, as the first Prime Minister of the federation and makes "a show piece of an appointment" to Dr. Ozimba as President of the federation. The potential divisiveness of the Governor's decision is apparent in lieu of their respective political ideologies, i.e., religious separatism versus Pan-Africanism. Therefore, the descent of the country into Civil War is inevitable, as it has been presaged. In the words of a Nigerian army colonel,

> "It is not an election but a time bomb. It will explode soon, you mark my words. How many of us are going to sit on our backsides and let this happen? Mallam Nguru Kano the first Nigerian Prime Minister indeed! This result is like playing Hamlet without the prince. Can you imagine a Nigerian government without the great Dr. Ozimba?"[4]

That it is the greed of the Europeans responsible for the ensuing blood bath is re-iterated throughout the novel. Debbie Ogedemgbe, daughter of the Minister of Finance, identifies Alan Grey, son of the former colonial governor, as the embodiment of mercantilism as he, in the interest of foreign trade, allies himself with both the Hausas and the Igbos in order to appear the enemy of neither.

The symbolic rape of the country, represented by the war, is also registered in the account of Captain Alan Grey's "sideline," that of acquiring African artifacts, "bronzes, carved elephant tusks and moulded animal figures which Western culture had dubbed 'primitive art,'" before the Nigerians discovered their true worth: "By the time Nigerians came to appreciate the worth of their own products, irreplaceable valuables would have been sold to adorn the homes of English aristocrats or rich Americans."[5]

Unfortunately, Emecheta's reductionist characterization has led to criticism of the kind leveled against Armah, namely, the charge of polemicism, as contained in a review of *Two Thousand Seasons* by S. Nyamfukudza. On the novel, Nyamfukudza has written:

> The message is relentlessly at the fore-front and we are much closer to the traditional tribal story teller, whose purpose is to educate and preserve the group's identity, history and traditions, than to any familiar novelistic form. . . . The theory and attempt are bold and admirable, but the resulting simplification and polarisation are an impoverishment of Armah's art.[6]

With respect to the work of Emecheta, *Destination Biafra,* according to Katherine Frank, sets in sharp relief the issues surrounding the debate over aesthetic criteria:

> How are we to judge a work which we find politically admirable and true but aesthetically simplistic, empty, or boring? What do we make of characters whose credos and pronouncements we endorse but whose human reality we find negligible? We are confronting here the vexed issue of commitment.[7]

The vacuousness of the characters that Frank has identified in her article "Women Without Men: The Feminist Novel in Africa" is best represented in the novel's collective group of politicians. Invariably, they are viewed as corrupt and self-serving. The fissure between them and the people they serve is reflected in their corpulence which is emblematic of their gluttony, or their pilfery of the nation's resources for personal aggrandizement. The Minister of Finance, Samuel Ogedemgbe, is described in terms reminiscent of Joe Koomson and Ababio, Densu's guardian, in Armah's *The Beautyful Ones Are Not Yet Born* and *The Healers,* respectively: "He tried to lie on his stomach, but it was not possible; he was too fat, the bed too soft, his surroundings too rich."[8]

Emecheta's brush-stroke delineation of Nigeria's politicians is evident in her portrayal of them at the state banquet in celebration of the country's independence. They are seen in the following unflattering terms: "Politicians congratulated each other and ate too much against the background of music played by the latest fashionable orchestra, though most of them were either too fat or too lazy to dance."[9]

The upshot of these fixed types in both Emecheta's and Armah's works is prosaicism. On this score, Derek Wright has observed that since the publication of *The Healers,* Armah has published only one other minor piece of fiction, a short story "Halfway to Nirvana," a creative drought which he attributes to "flagging inspiration and waning artistic execution." Wright also finds the latter works *Two Thousand*

Seasons and *The Healers* to be "laboured, repetitious, and overburdened with adjectives and high-sounding phrases which sometimes conceal illogicalities of thought."[10] The opening lines of *The Healers* are provided as evidential of the "supererogatory adjectival insistence":

> In the twentieth year of his life, a young man found himself at the centre of strange, extraordinary events. Someone was murdered--a youth exactly the same age as himself. The killing was done in a particularly bloody, brutal way. Those who saw the victim's butchered body agreed on one thing: the murderer acted from a fierce, passionate motive springing out of jealousy made hotter by pure, vindictive hate.

Wright goes on to theorize that the forced conclusions of Armah's historic fictions, the proclamation of victory and national unity in *Two Thousand Seasons* and *The Healers,* may be evidence of a critical cul-de-sac.

Interestingly enough, the "intellectual barrenness" of the creative artist in *The Woman Destroyed,* a collection of short stories by Simone de Beauvoir, is represented as the effects of aging. A Sorbonne professor in the short story "The Age of Discretion" publishes a "monumental" work on Rousseau and Montesquieu that advances critical methods that she has applied in her previous books; however, removed as they are from the contexts to which she had earlier applied them, they lose their adroitness. Hence, her new work represents no more than a "synthesis," or "a well-based restatement" of her previous works.[11]

On Simone de Beauvoir's own oeuvre, Toril Moi, in her work *Simone de Beauvoir: The Making of an Intellectual,* has opined that

> In my view, by the end of 1949, the year in which she published *The Second Sex,* Simone de Beauvoir had truly become Simone de Beauvoir: personally as well as professionally, she was 'made.' Her later life adds little to the repertoire of themes and obsessions established by this time: it is tempting to argue that *all* her major texts ceaselessly return to the period before 1950.[12]

At this writing, the argument of "stagnation" with respect to Ayi Kwei Armah may be premature, since it has been reported that he has completed a sixth novel, entitled "Osiris Rising: A Novel of Africa Past, Present and Future," that has yet to find a publisher.[13]

In the article "One Writer's Education," Armah had expressed his respect for persons who had "worked to create new realities," noting conversely the ineffectuality of the creative artist.[14] The recognition that words are no substitute for action accounts for the paralysis of Armah's fictional surrogate Solo in *Why Are We So Blest?* and may explain as well the Ayi Kwei Armah's decade-long silence.

Ode S. Ogede sheds additional light on the matter. He contends that the drawbacks of writing fiction in a largely analphabetic society may

have become increasingly evident to Armah. The awareness of the need
to reach the African public while constricted by a foreign medium has,
in fact, led writers such as Ngugi, Soyinka, and Ousmane to explore
drama. It has also led Ngugi wa Thiong'o to eschew English as "a
vehicle for [his] writing of plays, novels and short stories" and to adopt
instead Gikuyu, his mother tongue for same. Ngugi views his choice
of language as tantamount to a political stand; a means of restoring
harmony to the peoples of Africa whose linguistic estrangement has led
to a dissociation from both their experience and identity. Ngugi
compares the division caused by language to "separating the mind from
the body so that they are occupying two unrelated linguistic spheres in
the same person. On a larger social scale it is like producing a society
of bodiless heads and headless bodies."[15] Hence, one may agree
alongside Ogede that the recognition of the African writer's paradox of
communicating to the African working class in European languages that
Ngugi has found resolution for by the adoption of his mother tongue
possibly still dogs Armah and may explain his diminishing output.
Ogede has theorized:

> Armah expresses a lack of faith in the power of the written work but proceeds apace
> to plead the cause of writers. . . . These issues are part of the paradox of the
> African writer, who is conscious of the limitations imposed by the form within
> which he functions in his own kind of setting yet faces a situation in which no
> viable alternatives suggest themselves.[16]

In a similar vein, Ngugi has described the paralysis resultant from the
language dilemma of appealing to the African masses in European
languages: "Its quest was hampered by the very language choice, and
in its movement toward the people, it could only go up to that section
of the petty-bourgeoisie--the students, teachers, secretaries for instance--
still in closest touch with the people. It settled there, marking time,
caged within the linguistic fence of its colonial inheritance."[17]

In conclusion, it may be argued at this juncture that Ayi Kwei
Armah's literary career is a telling example of the enervation induced in
the African writer who, having heeded the clarion call of writers/critics
that the literature be engagé, nonetheless, finds himself compelled to
tread a mental tightrope in lieu of his unique circumstances--marketing
his work to European publishers while aiming it ostensibly at African
readers. Indeed, the quandary that Rand Bishop has described in his
work *African Literature, African Critics: The Forming of Critical
Standards, 1947-1966* could precipitate the kind of critical impasse that
seems to have affected the Ghanaian author Ayi Kwei Armah:

> African writers wanted to reach a Western audience but on their own terms; yet they
> were not in a position to dictate those terms. They had to write for a Western

publisher; they wanted to write for a Western audience; but they had also to write for an African critic who told them they should write for an African audience.[18]

1. Eustace Palmer, "Negritude Rediscovered: A Reading of the Recent Novels of Armah, Ngugi, and Soyinka." *International Fiction Review* 8, no. 1 (1981): 1-11.

2. Simone Schwarz-Bart, *Between Two Worlds*, trans. Barbara Bray (London: Heinemann, 1981), 50-51.

3. Charles Atangama Nama, "Aesthetics and Ideology in African and Afro-American Fiction: Ngugi wa Thiong'o, Ayi Kwei Armah, Toni Morrison and Richard Wright" (Ph.D. diss., State University of New York at Binghamton, 1984), 101.

4. Buchi Emecheta, *Destination Biafra* (London: Heinemann, 1982), 25.

5. Ibid., 6.

6. S. Nyamfukudza, "Drought & Rain," review of *Two Thousand Seasons*, by Ayi Kwei Armah, *New Statesman* 99 (March 7, 1980): 363.

7. Katherine Frank, "Women Without Men: The Feminist Novel in Africa." In *Women in African Literature Today* 15 (1987): 14-34.

8. Emecheta, 26.

9. Ibid., 39.

10. Derek Wright, *Ayi Kwei Armah's Africa: The Sources of His Fiction* (London: Hans Zell Publishers, 1989), 281.

11. Simone de Beauvoir, "The Age of Discretion," in *The Woman Destroyed*, trans. Patrick O'Brian (New York: G.P. Putnam's Sons, 1969), 62.

12. Toril Moi, *Simone de Beauvoir: The Making of an Intellectual Woman* (Cambridge: Blackwell Publishers, 1994), 6.

13. "Publication News," *African Literature Association Bulletin* 22, no. 2 (spring 1996): 30.

14. Ayi Kwei Armah, "One Writer's Education," *West Africa*, 26 August 1985, 1752-53.

15. Ngugi wa Thiong'o, *Decolonising the Mind: The Politics of Language in African Literature.* (London: Heinemann, 1986), 28.

16. Ode S. Ogede, "Angled Shots and Reflections: On the Literary Essays of Ayi Kwei Armah," *World Literature Today* 66, no. 3 (1992): 443.

17. Ngugi, 21-22.

18. Rand Bishop, *African Literature, African Critics: The Forming of Critical Standards, 1947-1966* (New York: Greenwood Press, 1988), 54.

A Selected Bibliography

Primary Sources:

Fiction by Ayi Kwei Armah:

Armah, Ayi Kwei. *The Beautyful Ones Are Not Yet Born.* New York: Houghton Mifflin, 1968.
---. *Fragments.* New York: Collier Books, 1969.
---. "Halfway to Nirvana." *West Africa,* 24 September 1984, 1947-48.
---. *The Healers.* London: Heinemann, 1978.
---. "The Offal Kind." *Harper's Magazine,* January 1969, 79-84.
---. *Two Thousand Seasons.* London: Heinemann, 1979.
---. *Why Are We So Blest?.* New York: Anchor Press, 1973.
---. "Yaw Manu's Charm." *Atlantic,* May 1968, 89-95.

Articles by Ayi Kwei Armah:

Armah, Ayi Kwei. "Africa and the Francophone Dream." *West Africa,* 28 April 1986, 884-85.
---. "African Socialism: Utopian or Scientific?." *Présence Africaine* 64 (1964): 6-30.
---. "The Caliban Complex." Parts 1 and 2. *West Africa,* 18 and 25 March 1985, 521-22, 570-71.
---. "Chaka." *Black World* 24 (February 1975).
---. "The Festival Syndrome." *West Africa,* 15 April 1985, 726-27.
---. "Flood and Famine, Drought and Glut." *West Africa,* 30 September 1985, 2011-12.
---. "The Lazy School of Literary Criticism." *West Africa,* 25 February 1985, 353-54.
---. "Masks and Marx: The Marxist Ethos vis-à-vis African Revolutionary Theory and Praxis." *Présence Africaine* 131 (1984): 35-65.
---. "A Mystification: African Independence Revalued." *Pan-African Journal* 2, no. 2 (spring 1969): 141-51.
---. "One Writer's Education." *West Africa,* 26 August 1985, 1752-53.
---. "Our Language Problem." *West Africa,* 29 April 1985, 831-32.
---. "The Oxygen of Translation." *West Africa,* 11 February 1985, 262-63.
---. "The Third World Hoax." *West Africa,* 25 August 1986, 1781-82.
---. "Sundiata, An Epic of Old Mali." *Black World* 25, no. 7, (May 1974).

---. "The Teaching of Creative Writing." *West Africa,* 20 May 1985, 994-95.

---. "Writers as Professionals." *West Africa,* 11 August 1986, 1680.

Primary Works by Other Authors:

Achebe, Chinua. *No Longer at Ease.* London: Heinemann, 1960.

---. *Things Fall Apart.* London: Heinemann, 1959.

Beauvoir de, Simone. *Adieux: A Farewell to Sartre.* Trans. Patrick O'Brian. New York: Pantheon, 1984.

---. *The Mandarins.* Trans. Leonard M. Friedman. New York: W.W. Norton, 1991.

---. *The Prime of Life: The Autobiography of Simone de Beauvoir, 1929-1944.* Trans. Peter Green. New York: Paragon, 1992.

---. *The Second Sex.* Trans. H.M. Parshley. New York: Alfred A. Knopf, 1952.

---. *The Woman Destroyed.* Trans. Patrick O'Brian. New York: G.P. Putnam's Sons, 1969.

---. *She Came to Stay.* New York: Norton, 1954.

Camus, Albert. *The Just Assassins.* In his *Caligula and Three Other Plays.* Trans. Stuart Gilbert. New York: Alfred A. Knopf, 1967.

---. *The Myth of Sisyphus and Other Essays.* Trans. Justin O'Brien. New York: Alfred A. Knopf, 1955.

---. "Neither Victims nor Executioners." Trans. Dwight Macdonald. *Politics* 4, no. 4 (July-August 1947): 141-47.

---. *The Rebel: An Essay on Man in Revolt.* Trans. Anthony Bower. New York: Alfred A. Knopf, 1956.

---. *Resistance, Rebellion, and Death.* Trans. Justin O'Brien. New York: Alfred A. Knopf, 1960.

---. *The Stranger.* Trans. Stuart Gilbert. New York: Alfred A. Knopf, 1946.

Emecheta, Buchi. *Destination Biafra.* London: Heinemann, 1982.

Lamming, George. *In the Castle of My Skin.* New York: Schocken, 1983.

Sartre, Jean-Paul. *The Age of Reason.* Trans. Eric Sutton. New York: Alfred A. Knopf, 1947.

---. *Being and Nothingness: An Essay in Phenomenological Ontology.* Translated and introduced by Hazel Barnes. New York: Philosophical Library, 1956.

---. "The Childhood of a Leader." In his *Intimacy and Other Stories.* Trans. Lloyd Alexander. New York: New Directions, 1948.

---. *Dirty Hands.* In his *No Exit and Three Other Plays.* Trans. L. Abel. New York: Alfred A. Knopf, 1948.

---. *Existential Psychoanalysis.* Translated and introduced by Hazel Barnes. New York: Philosophical Library, 1953.

---. *Existentialism and Humanism.* Trans. Philip Mairet. London: Methuen, 1948.

---. "An Explication of *The Stranger.*" In *Camus: A Collection of Critical Essays,* edited by Germaine Brée, 108-21. Englewood, N.J.: Prentice-Hall, 1962. Originally published in *Situations* 1 (1947).

---. *Nausea.* Trans. Lloyd Alexander. New York: New Directions, 1964.

---. *No Exit.* In his *No Exit and Three Other Plays.* Trans. Stuart Gilbert. New York: Alfred A. Knopf, 1948.

---. Preface to *The Wretched of the Earth,* by Frantz Fanon. Trans. Constance Farrington. New York: Grove Press, 1968.

---. "The Room." In his *Intimacy and Other Stories.* Trans. Lloyd Alexander. New York: New Directions, 1948.

Schwarz-Bart. Simone. *Between Two Worlds.* Trans. Barbara Bray. Heinemann, 1981.

Secondary Sources:

Abrahams, Cecil. "Perspectives on Africa." *Canadian Journal of African Studies* 2 (1977): 355-59.

Achebe, Chinua. *Morning Yet on Creation Day.* New York: Anchor: Doubleday Press, 1975.

Amuta, Chidi. "Portraits of the Contemporary African Artist in Armah's Novels." *World Literature Written in English* 21 (autumn 1982): 467-76.

---. "The Revolutionary Imperative in the Contemporary African Novel: Ngugi's *Petals of Blood* and Armah's *The Healers.*" *Commonwealth Novel in English* 3 (fall 1990): 130-42.

Anyidoho, Kofi. "Historical Realism and the Visionary Ideal: Ayi Kwei Armah's *Two Thousand Seasons.*" *Ufahamu* 11, no. 2 (1981-82): 108-30.

Ayuk, G. Ojong. "The Lust for Material Well-Being in *The Beautyful Ones Are Not Yet Born* and *Fragments* by Ayi Kwei Armah." *Présence Africaine* 132 (1984): 33-43.

Bair, Deirdre. *Simone de Beauvoir: A Biography.* New York: Summit, 1990.

Barnes, Hazel. *Sartre.* New York: J.B. Lippincott, 1973.

---. *Humanistic Existentialism: The Literature of Possibility.* Lincoln: University of Nebraska Press, 1959.

Barrett, William. *Irrational Man: A Study in Existential Philosophy.* New York: Doubleday, 1952.

Berger, Roger A. "Ngugi's Comic Vision." *Research in African Literatures* 20, no. 1 (spring 1989): 1-25.

Bishop, Rand. *African Literature, African Critics: The Forming of Critical Standards, 1947-1966.* New York: Greenwood Press, 1988.

Booth, James. "Why Are We So Blest? and the Limits of Metaphor." *Journal of Commonwealth Literature* 15, no. 1 (August 1980): 50-64.

Brée, Germaine. *Camus and Sartre: Crisis and Commitment.* New York: Dell, 1972.

Brombart, Victor. *The Intellectual Hero: Studies in the French Novel (1880-1955).* New York: J.B. Lippincott, 1960.

Carew, Jan. "African Literature--From the Breath of Gods." Review of *Why Are We So Blest?*, by Ayi Kwei Armah. *The New York Times Book Review*, 14 March 1972, 7.

Chakava, Henry. "Ayi Kwei Armah and a Commonwealth of Souls." In *Standpoints on African Literature: A Critical Anthology*, edited by Chris Wanjala. 197-208. Nairobi: East African Literature Bureau, 1973.

Chantler, Clyde. *The Ghana Story.* London: Linden Press, 1971.

Cheatwood, Kiarri. Review of *Why Are We So Blest?*, by Ayi Kwei Armah. *Black World* 23, no. 5 (March 1974): 85-90.

Chinweizu, Onwuchekwa Jemie, and Ihechukwu Madubuike. *Toward the Decolonization of African Literature. Vol. 1. African Fiction and Poetry and Their Critics.* Washington, D.C.: Howard UP, 1983.

Cohen-Solal, Annie. *Sartre: A Life.* Trans. Anna Cancogni. New York: Pantheon, 1987.

Collins, Harold. "Founding a New National Literature." *Critique: Studies in Modern Fiction* 4 (1960-61): 17-28.

---. "The Ironic Imagery in Armah's *The Beautyful Ones Are Not Yet Born*: The Putrescent Vision." *World Literature Written in English* 20 (1971): 37-50.

Cranston, Maurice. *Jean-Paul Sartre.* New York: Grove Press, 1962.

Cruickshank, John. *Albert Camus and the Literature of Revolt.* New York: Galaxy, 1960.

Davidson, Basil. *The African Slave Trade: Precolonial History 1450-1850.* Boston: Little, Brown, 1961.

Emenyonu, Ernest. "Who Does Flora Nwapa Write For?." *African Literature Today* 7 (1975): 28-33.

Fage, J.D. *A History of West Africa: An Introductory Survey*. 4th ed. Cambridge: Cambridge UP, 1969.

Fanon, Frantz. *Black Skin, White Masks*. Trans. Constance Farrington. New York: Grove Press, 1967.

---. *The Wretched of the Earth*. Trans. Constance Farrington. New York: Grove Press, 1963.

Fenton, Leslie L. "Symbolism and Theme in Peters' *The Second Round* and Armah's *The Beautyful Ones Are Not Yet Born*." *Pan-African Journal* 6, no. 1 (spring 1973): 83-90.

Folarin, Margaret. "An Additional Comment on Ayi Kwei Armah's *The Beautyful Ones Are Not Yet Born*." *African Literature Today* 5 (1971): 116-29.

Fraser, Robert. "The American Background in *Why Are We So Blest?*." *African Literature Today* 9 (1978): 39-46.

---. *The Novels of Ayi Kwei Armah*. London: Heinemann, 1980.

Gikandi, Simon. *Reading the African Novel*. Portsmouth, NH: Heinemann, 1987.

Greene, Norman N. *Jean-Paul Sartre: The Existentialist Ethic*. Ann Arbor: University of Michigan Press, 1960.

Griffiths, Gareth. *A Double Exile: African and West Indian Writing Between Two Cultures*. London: Marion Boyars, 1978.

---. "Structure and Image in Kwei Armah's *The Beautyful Ones Are Not Yet Born*." *Studies in Black Literature* 2, no. 2 (1971): 1-9.

Hanna, Thomas. "Albert Camus: Man in Revolt." In *Existential Philosophers: Kierkegaard to Merleau-Ponty*, edited by George Schrader. 331-367. New York: McGraw-Hill, 1967.

Irele, Abiola. "The Criticism of Modern African Literature." In *Perspectives on African Literature*, edited by Christopher Heywood. 9-30. New York: Africana Publishing, 1971.

"Is Blindness Best?." Review of *Fragments*, by Ayi Kwei Armah. *Time*, 2 February 1970, 72-73.

Iyasere, Solomon. "African Critics on African Literature: A Study of Misplaced Hostility." *Journal of Modern African Studies* 12 (September 1974): 514-19.

---. "The Place of Oral Tradition in the Criticism of African Literature." *Books Abroad: An International Literary Quarterly* (winter 1975): 50-56.

James, Adeola. Review of *Idu*, by Flora Nwapa. *African Literature Today* 5 (1971): 150-53.

Johnson, Joyce. "The Promethean 'Factor' in Ayi Kwei Armah's *Fragments* and *Why Are We So Blest?*." *World Literature Written in English* 21 (autumn 1982): 497-512.

Johnson, Lemuel. "The Middle Passage in African Literature: Wole Soyinka, Yambo Ouologuem, Ayi Kwei Armah." *African Literature Today* 11 (1980): 62-84.

Jones, Eldred. "Locale and Universe--Three Nigerian Novels." *Journal of Commonwealth Literature* 3 (1967): 127-31.

---. Review of *The Beautyful Ones Are Not Yet Born*, by Ayi Kwei Armah. *African Literature Today: Journal of Explanatory Criticism* 3 (1969): 55-57.

Kibera, Leonard. "Pessimism and the African Novelist: Ayi Kwei Armah's *The Beautyful Ones Are Not Yet Born.*" *Journal of Commonwealth Literature* 14, no. 1 (1979): 64-73.

Komolo, Ejiet. "Armah's Cargo Mentality: A Critical Review of *Fragments.*" *Dhana* 4, no. 2 (1974): 88-90.

Lafarge, René. *Jean-Paul Sartre: His Philosophy.* Trans. Marina Smyth-Kok. Notre Dame: University of Notre Dame Press, 1967.

Larson, Charles. "Ayi Kwei Armah's Vision of African Reciprocity." Review of *Two Thousand Seasons,* by Ayi Kwei Armah. *Africa Today* 21, no. 2 (March 1974): 117-19.

---. Review of *Why Are We So Blest?,* by Ayi Kwei Armah. *Saturday Review,* 31 January 1970, 40.

Lawson, William. *The Western Scar: The Theme of the Been-to in West African Fiction.* Athens, Ohio: Ohio UP, 1982.

Lazarus, Neil. "The Implications of Technique in Ayi Kwei Armah's *The Healers.*" *Research in African Literatures* 13 (winter 1982): 488-98.

---. "Pessimism of the Intellect, Optimism of the Will: A Reading of Ayi Kwei Armah's *The Beautyful Ones Are Not Yet Born.*" *Research in African Literatures* 18, no. 2 (1987): 137-75.

---. Review of *The Novels of Ayi Kwei Armah,* by Robert Fraser. *Research in African Literatures* 15, no. 3 (1984): 444-47.

Lindfors, Bernth. "Armah's Histories." *African Literature Today* 11 (1980): 85-96.

lo Liyong, Taban. "Ayi Kwei Armah in Two Moods." *The Journal of Commonwealth Literature* 25 (August 1991): 1-18.

Lobb, Edward. "Personal and Political Fate in Armah's *Why Are We So Blest?*" *World Literature Written in English* 19, no. 1 (1980): 5-19.

Madsen, Axel. *Hearts and Minds: The Common Journey of Simone de Beauvoir and Jean-Paul Sartre.* New York: William Morrow and Company, 1977.

Mahood, Molly. Review of *Fragments,* by Ayi Kwei Armah. *Saturday Review,* 31 January 1970, 40.

Maja-Pearce, Adewale. "Just Another Sick Book." Review of *Why Are We So Blest?*, by Ayi Kwei Armah. *Okike* 23 (1983): 133-36.

Manser, Anthony. *Sartre: A Philosophic Study.* London: Athlone Press, 1966.

Maquet, Albert. *Albert Camus: The Invincible Summer.* New York: George Braziller, 1958.

Masters, Brian. *Sartre: A Study.* London: Heinemann, 1974.

McCall, Dorothy. *The Theatre of Jean-Paul Sartre.* New York: Columbia UP, 1967.

Meredith, Martin. "The Shattered Dream: The Sorry State of Ghana, 25 Years After the High Hopes of Independence." *The Sunday Times Magazine*, 7 March 1982.

Moi, Toril. *Simone de Beauvoir: The Making of an Intellectual Woman.* Cambridge: Blackwell Publishers, 1994.

Moore, Gerald. "Armah's Second Novel." Review of *Fragments*, by Ayi Kwei Armah. *Journal of Commonwealth Literature* 9, no. 1 (August 1974): 69-71.

Murra, John. "The Unconscious of a Race." Review of *The Palm-Wine Drinkard* and *My Life in the Bush*, by Amos Tutuola. *Nation* 179 (September 1954): 261-62.

Nama, Charles Atangana. "Aesthetics and Ideology in African and Afro-American Fiction: Ngugi wa Thiong'o, Ayi Kwei Armah, Toni Morrison and Richard Wright." Ph.D. diss., State University of New York at Binghamton, 1984.

Ngugi wa Thiong'o. *Decolonising the Mind: The Politics of Language in African Literature.* London: Heinemann, 1986.

Nkolim, Charles E. "Dialectic as Form: Pejorism in the Novels of Armah." *African Literature Today: Retrospect and Prospect* 10 (1979): 207-23.

Noble, R.W. "A Beautyful Novel." Review of *The Beautyful Ones Are Not Yet Born*, by Ayi Kwei Armah. *Journal of Commonwealth Literature* 9, no. 2 (1970): 117-19.

Nwahunanya, Chinyere. "A Vision of the Ideal: Armah's *Two Thousand Seasons*" *Modern Fiction Studies* 37 (autumn 1991): 549-60.

Nwoga, D. Ibe. "The Limitations of Universal Critical Criteria." *Dalhousie Review* 53 (1973-74): 608-30.

Nyamfukudza, S. "Drought and Rain." Review of *Two Thousand Seasons* and *The Healers*, by Ayi Kwei Armah, and *The Novels of Ayi Kwei Armah*, by Robert Fraser. *New Statesman*, 7 March 1980: 362-63.

144   *Existential Fiction*

Obiechina, E.N. Review of *The Beautyful Ones Are Not Yet Born,* by Ayi Kwei Armah. *Okike: A Nigerian Journal of New Writing* 1 (1971): 49-53.

Obumselu, Ben. "Marx, Politics and the African Novel." *Twentieth Century Studies* 10 (December 1973): 107-27.

Ogede, Ode S. "Angled Shots and Reflections: On the Literary Essays of Ayi Kwei Armah." *World Literature Today* 66 (summer 1992): 339-444.

---. "Ayi Kwei Armah in America: The Question of Identity in *Why Are We So Blest?*" *Ariel: A Review of International English Literature* 21 (October 1990): 49-66.

---. "Patterns of Decadence, Visions of Regeneration in Armah's *Fragments.*" *Modern Fiction Studies* 37 (autumn 1991): 529-48.

---. "The Rhetoric of Revolution in Armah's *The Healers:* Form as Experience." *African Studies Review* 36 (April 1993): 43-58.

Ogungbesan, Kolawole. "Symbol and Meaning in *The Beautyful Ones Are Not Yet Born.*" *African Literature Today* 7 (1975): 93-110.

Okpewho, Isidore. "Myth and Modern Fiction: Armah's *Two Thousand Seasons.*" *African Literature Today* 13 (1983): 1-22.

Palmer, Eustace. "The Criticism of African Fiction: Its Nature and Function." *International Fiction Review* 1 (July 1974): 112-19.

---. *The Growth of the African Novel.* London: Heinemann, 1979.

---. *An Introduction to the African Novel: A Critical Study of Thirteen Books.* New York: Africana Publishing, 1972.

---. "Negritude Rediscovered: A Reading of the Recent Novels of Armah, Ngugi, and Soyinka." *International Fiction Review* 8, no. 1 (1981): 1-11.

Peck, Richard. "Hermits and Saviors, Osagyefos and Healers: Artists and Intellectuals in the Works of Ngugi and Armah." *Research in African Literatures* 20 (spring 1989): 26-49.

Petersen, Kirsten Holst. "Loss and Frustration: An Analysis of A.K. Armah's *Fragments.*" *Kunapipi* 1, no. 1 (1979): 53-65.

---. "The New Way." Review of *Two Thousand Seasons,* by Ayi Kwei Armah. *World Literature Written in English* 15, no. 2 (November 1976): 330-35.

Pieterse, Cosmo and Dennis Duerden. *African Writers Talking: A Collection of Radio Interviews.* New York: Africana Publishing, 1972.

Pollmann, Leo. *Sartre and Camus: Literature of Existence.* New York: Frederick Ungar, 1970.

Priebe, Richard. "The Development of a Mythic Consciousness in West African Literature." Ph.D. diss., University of Texas at Austin, 1973.

"Publication News." *African Literature Association Bulletin* 22, no. 2 (spring 1996): 30-34.

Rao, K. Damodar. *The Novels of Ayi Kwei Armah*. New Delhi: Prestige, 1993.

Review of *Two Thousand Seasons*, by Ayi Kwei Armah. *Ebony* (January 1980): 24.

Sackey, Edward. "Oral Tradition and the African Novel." *Modern Fiction Studies* 37 (autumn 1991): 389-407.

Sekyi-Otu, Ato. "Toward Anoa . . . Not Back to Anoa": The Grammar of Revolutionary Homecoming in *Two Thousand Seasons.*" *Research in African Literatures* 18, no. 2 (1987): 192-214.

Simonse, Simon. "African Literature Between Nostalgia and Utopia: African Novels Since 1953 in the Light of the Modes-of-Production Approach." *Research in African Literatures* 13 (winter 1982): 451-87.

Snyder, Emile. "New Directions in African Writings." *Pan-African Journal* 5 (1972): 253-61.

Soyinka, Wole. *Myth, Literature and the African World*. Cambridge: Cambridge University Press, 1976.

Spencer, Norman Albritton. "Political Consciousness and Commitment in Modern African Literature: A Study of the Novels of Ayi Kwei Armah." Ph.D. diss., State University of New York at Stony Brook, 1985.

Steele, Shelby. "Existentialism in the Novels of Ayi Kwei Armah." *Obsidian: Black Literature in Review* 3 (spring 1977): 5-13.

Stern, Alfred. *Sartre: His Philosophy and Existential Psychoanalysis*. 2nd rev. ed. New York: Delacorte, 1967.

Thody, Philip. *Albert Camus 1913-1960*. London: Harrish Hamilton, 1961.

Tucker, Martin. "Tragedy of a Been-to." *The New Republic* 162, no. 31 (January 1970): 24-26.

Walker, William A., Jr. "Major Ghanaian Fiction in English: A Study of the Novels of Ayi Kwei Armah and Kofi Awoonor." Ph.D. diss., University of Texas at Austin, 1975.

Wilks, Ivor. *Asante in the Nineteenth Century: The Structure and Evolution of a Political Order*. London: Cambridge University Press, 1975.

Wright, Derek. "Armah's Ghana Revisited: History and Fiction." *The International Fiction Review* 12, no. 1 (1985): 23-27.

---. *Ayi Kwei Armah's Africa. The Sources of His Fiction*. London: Hans Zell, 1989.

---. "Flux and Form: The Geography of Time in *The Beautyful Ones Are Not Yet Born.*" *Ariel* 17, no. 2 (1986): 63-77.

---. *"Fragments:* The Akan Background." *Research in African Literatures* 18, no. 2 (1987): 176-91.

---. "Motivation and Motif: The Carrier Rite in Ayi Kwei Armah's *The Beautyful Ones Are Not Yet Born." English Studies in Africa* 28, no. 2 (1985): 119-33.

---. "Requiems for Revolutions: Race-Sex Archetypes in Two African Novels." *Modern Fiction Studies* 35 (spring 1989): 55-68.

---. "Totalitarian Rhetoric: Some Aspects of Metaphor in *The Beautyful Ones Are Not Yet Born." Critique: Studies in Contemporary Fiction* 30 (spring 1989): 210-20.

Wright, Richard. *Black Boy (American Hunger): A Record of Childhood and Youth.* New York: Harper Perennial, 1993.

Index

The Author

Tommie Lee Jackson holds a B.A. from Paine College, Augusta, Georgia, and M.A. and Ph.D. degrees from the University of Nebraska-Lincoln. She is currently a professor of English at St. Cloud State University, St. Cloud, Minnesota, where she teaches African-American, African, and Caribbean literature.